All About

■ the ■

dixie
chicks

All About
the
dixie
chicks

Ace Collins

St. Martin's Griffin

New York

ISBN 0-312-24705-2

First Edition: September 1999

10 9 8 7 6 5 4 3 2 1

Book design by Judith Stagnitto Abbate/ABBATE DESIGN

Dedicated to Barbara Mandrell, an entertainer who redefined women's potential in Nashville and took country music to the country via the *Barbara Mandrell and the Mandrell Sisters* television show,

and Alabama, the artists who opened the door to country music for millions of new fans and scores of bands who played country, not rock.

Contents

All About
the
dixie
chicks

1

Texas Yankees
with
Bluegrass Roots

Though they're now considered one of the most celebrated groups in the long and storied history of Texas music, the foundation of the musical revolution that came to fruition in the Dixie Chicks first saw the light of day a long way from the Lone Star State. On October 12, 1969, schoolteachers Paul and Barbara Erwin welcomed their second child into the world in Pittsfield, Massachusetts. On that New England fall day, daughter Martie joined her older sister, Julie, as the focal point of the Erwin household. Almost three years later, on August 16, 1972, another sister, Emily, made the Erwin siblings a trio.

In the modern world of marketing, it is constantly said that timing and location are everything. There can be little doubt that if the Erwin girls had been born two decades earlier or had grown up in New England, the Dixie Chicks would never have surfaced, first on the streets of Dallas and later on stages around the world. The trio that in two short years has become the best-selling female country music group of all time would have never come together at all in Boston or New York. Yet fate, often the major player in elevating a performer from obscurity to stardom, played a hand in Martie and Emily's favor. Not only did they find themselves in the right atmosphere for creating a new sound, thanks to the hard work of another group of sisters and a band, when the girls had evolved to a place where they were ready for a shot at the big time, the world of country music was ready to give them their chance.

Not long after the arrival of their third child, the Erwins followed the example set by millions of other Yankees, by packing their bags, escaping the snow, and heading south. The family settled in Dallas, Texas. Famous worldwide as the home of television's Ewing family, the city, with its sprawling suburbs and rapid expansion, was morphing cowboys with businessmen and in a tax-friendly environment was showing America just how much Texas had changed since the days of Jim Bowie and Sam Houston. The Erwins would fall in love with the city, its people, and its culture.

Music had always been an important facet of Paul and Barbara Erwin's lives, and the couple was bound and determined to make sure it was a part of their daughters' lives as well. With the possible exceptions of Memphis and Nashville, the family couldn't have picked a better place to experience the full range of musical genres.

The Dallas–Fort Worth area had been a hotbed of

rock, blues, gospel, and country for decades. In honky-tonks across the area, some of the best bands in the world pumped out a constant stream of music that echoed down dark alleys and up well-traveled streets. Influenced not only by the western culture of the region, but by the wide mix of ethnic groups who had first settled the state, DFW (Dallas–Fort Worth) music was part Buddy Holly, a taste of Stevie Ray Vaughan, a dose of V. O. Stamps, a portion of Bob Wills, a bit of Jim Reeves, and a pinch of Ernest Tubb. This was the area that had first embraced the likes of Elvis Presley, George Jones, and the Stamps Quartet. DFW turned out in droves for not only country and rock but blues and swing. Scores of big-band musicians and singers started here, as did the likes of Ray Price and Lefty Frizzell. No matter where you were from, no matter what your taste, on any given night you could easily find your musical niche in the metroplex.

Yet the music that would first come to shape the lives of Martie and Emily Erwin was not the eclectic mix found in clubs, or the country and rock played on the radio; rather, it was the grand strains of the classics played by the local highbrow community. It was in large concert halls that Paul and Barbara first exposed their daughters to the beauty of a symphony. From this early indoctrination, the two educators then eased their girls into learning at least one of the instruments that made up the orchestra.

The violin came first. Taught the Suzuki method, a musical training regimen first developed in Japan for very young children, the girls were given the opportunity to sport their talents on songs such as "Twinkle, Twinkle, Little Star." Perhaps because it's not a part of the public-school curriculum in most areas, the lack of passion for classical music in the United States has always put American music teachers behind their European and Asian counterparts. While the Suzuki system remains one of the best and most popular teaching platforms in the world, in truth most children last only a few months or years before dropping out to devote their time to soccer, T-ball, or dance. In Texas, where a majority of the population looks at a violin and thinks fiddle, it was especially difficult to keep children focused on the instrument.

Yet with the Erwin girls, the Suzuki method took root and grew. Barbara Erwin was not going to pay for the expensive lessons without making sure the girls devoted daily time to practice. Every day, aided by an old egg timer, she forced Martie and Emily to practice hard until they were finally saved by the timer's bell. Over the course of a few months, the forced practice sessions became a musical celebration of life as the girls began to thrive on the training. It would be Suzuki that first uncovered the girls deep passion for music. Almost before learning to read, the younger two Erwin girls were hooked on playing.

While watching her daughters perform with a symphony orchestra might have been a deeply held dream for Barbara, the culture that surrounded the girls in DFW quickly quashed that vision. Yet it took a little help from their dad, too. It might have been classical music Martie and Emily heard at the symphony and in the Suzuki practice halls, but it was the bluegrass music that they were exposed to when their father took them to several country music shows that took root in their souls. Slowly the girls began to add a touch of "Faded Love" and "Turkey in the

Straw" to the Suzuki course structure. Before long they were playing as much fiddle as violin. Yet even this move to country music would have probably proved useless if country music hadn't just begun to open the door to women.

In the coming 1980s, at about the time the Erwins had settled into Texas and the girls had begun school, another group of Texas sisters was storming the national airwaves, playing every musical instrument that they could lay their hands on. Like Martie and Emily, Barbara Mandrell, born on Christmas Day 1948, was a child prodigy who came from a musical family. Already performing at shows at the age of six in her family band, by her teens Barbara had not only toured much of the West Coast and played Las Vegas with Patsy Cline and Johnny Cash, but was now often joined by her younger sisters on USO tours in Europe and Vietnam. Long before she obtained her driver's license, the incredibly beautiful blonde was a seasoned professional.

When she arrived in Nashville — Music City — at the age of twenty in 1968, Mandrell didn't look much like the revolutionary leader who would fire the first shot in a war that would open a huge musical door for female country acts. Yet as she began to make the rounds and meet music-business movers and shakers, her spirit and vision started to appear. She was not just a singer, like the other females of her day; she was a complete musician and entertainer. She played a dozen instruments, several of them well enough to earn a spot in major bands; carried a dynamic and forceful presence on stage; and, like the Erwin girls, had a background in all types of musical genres. As Nashville quickly discovered, Mandrell's talents may have been wrapped in a diminutive five-foot package, but this Texan was one of the most explosive forces to ever migrate to the Tennessee music scene.

Within a year of landing a record contract, Mandrell was bent on not only making hits, but redefining women's roles in country music. She would be the person to finally set the women's movement on fire in Nashville and push the industry past just considering women as "girl singers." To accomplish this lofty goal, Barbara constantly pushed the envelope. She sang cheating songs where the woman, not the man, cheated! That was unheard of then. No one did that! She used rhythm-and-blues numbers in both the recording studio and in live shows—another concept frowned upon in Nashville. Today, with Shania Twain, Dena Carter, and Faith Hill oozing sex appeal and on-the-edge lyrics, listening to Barbara's songs would hardly be startling, but in the 1970s, when even Dolly Parton didn't show cleavage, what Barbara did and sang about were indeed groundbreaking.

Maybe even more important than her musical selection, subject, and style was Mandrell's determination to not be judged *just* against other female acts. Particularly during her live shows, Barbara declared her right to go it against the men. Mandrell did not want to be the opening act for a male singer; she wanted to headline. No country-music woman had ever dared even ask to be the closer. Not even Patsy Cline was given that right. Yet through hard work and determination, Mandrell would not just headline, but win back-to-back Country Music Association Entertainer of the Year Awards in 1980 and 1981 and nine annual

People's Choice Awards. In other words, she was deemed the best entertainer regardless of gender in country music and recognized as the nation's top female act in any category or genre. So Mandrell was becoming not just a star in Nashville; she was emerging as a dominant force in all of popular music. Yet what made her all these things was not as much country music as it was family ties and television.

NBC television's chief operating officer, Fred Silverman, caught Barbara and her sisters, Louise and Irlene, on *The Mike Douglas Show.* Their spontaneous musical combustion had won them a standing ovation from Douglas and his audiences. The sisters had also frozen Silverman in his seat. Silverman ordered a videotape of the program and watched it several more times, then called Barbara's father and manager, Irby Mandrell. At Barbara's Hendersonville, Tennessee, home, he met with Irby and the sisters and hammered out a deal for a new network variety show. Within months of that initial meeting, Barbara, Louise, and Irlene were the "Sweethearts of Saturday Night." In a very real sense, the Mandrells gave the Erwins a helping hand even before the Dallas kids knew they needed one. They did it by making country music the music of all of America.

Country music variety had been tried many times before by network television. Jimmy Dean's and Johnny Cash's shows had been successful in the fifties, sixties, and early seventies. Yet while the ratings were solid, neither of them had brought many new converts to country music. Record and concert sales had not jumped all over the board. Other country giants, like Dolly Parton, had tried and flopped on television. Yet Barbara was different from all the other country acts in both her ability to sustain an audience and the demographics of those thirty million weekly viewers who watched her.

Mandrell's show was an instant hit. Not only would *Barbara Mandrell and the Mandrell Sisters* earn great ratings in 1980–82, but it would pull those ratings from all age groups. Teens and preteens who had never heard of Roy Acuff or Charlie Pride were tuning in each week to watch Barbara, Louise, and Irlene and their special guests. In the process these kids were meeting the era's hottest new country stars and being inspired to pick up instruments and try to take country music another step forward.

Martie and Emily Erwin, like millions of others, often caught the Mandrells' television show. The sisters, just beginning their first ginger-steps into the musical world, couldn't have known that Barbara, Louise, and Irlene were opening doors for them. Of course, no one else in Nashville or Los Angeles realized the long-term effects the show was having, either. Even the millions who went to record stores to buy their first country LPs had not come to a full realization as to why they were tuning in and turning on to country music. Barbara, Louise, and Irlene didn't look like refugees from *Hee Haw* — they were too cool — and the music they performed didn't seem like generic country. For the first time even teens outside the South could listen to country music without being teased or ridiculed by their peers. The Mandrells' television show was an important step in bringing new fans to country music. Yet they themselves would never fully benefit from this new way of thinking, unlike Martie and Emily when they were finally recognized by Nashville.

While the Mandrells opened the door for country girl groups and exposed the nation to a new sound, it was a male act that grabbed country's new popularity and turned things upside down. Just like the Dixie Chicks would struggle in the early and mid-1990s, two decades earlier Young Country, a unique band with a new sound, would gain local acceptance but struggle to gain any kind of national acclaim. But after a name change it was Young Country that would complete what Barbara Mandrell and her sisters started, bringing country music to a younger audience and presenting it on a national level.

When Randy Owen, Jeff Cook, Teddy Gentry, and Mark Herndon, the southern band that began life as Young Country, made their national television network debut on *Barbara Mandrell and the Mandrell Sisters*, they created a major sensation. Though no one fully appreciated their impact at the time, the group would radically alter the way country music sounded and the money the industry generated. Almost by themselves, Alabama — their new moniker — took country music to the big time at the box office.

Alabama would not only become the first successful commercial country music band since Bob Wills and the Texas Playboys, but would also revolutionize the genre. As they scored chart-topping hit after hit, teenagers and college kids began to flock to their concerts and buy their records. As Alabama began to churn out gold records and rack up unheard-of sales and awards, teens and young adults were buying country music albums and singles by the millions. Maybe most importantly for the Erwin girls, even though they didn't know it then, with Mandrell and Alabama Nashville was being forced to realize the full potential of women and the fact that being in a band didn't automatically make you a rocker or a relic from the past.

It would be years before the impact of Mandrell and Alabama was fully realized. For the moment, *Barbara Mandrell and the Mandrell Sisters* just made life a great deal easier for parents trying to get their children to practice music, and Alabama opened the door to making country more fun. Yet with role models who could play, sing, dance, and headline their own shows, girls finally had a reason to dream of playing country music and being stars on the same level as men. And some might even have thought about joining a band and playing guitar.

With the new country-rock sounds of Alabama and all the musical influences that pumped up and down the streets of Dallas, it may seem odd that the Erwin girls chose to embrace a style of playing rarely heard in Texas. Bluegrass was the music of Kentucky and Tennessee; it was played by old-timers such as Bill Monroe and Earl Scruggs; it received its limited exposure at small music festivals, on *Grand Ole Opry*, or in reruns of *The Beverly Hillbillies*. Yet moving from classical fiddle to songs such as "Cripple Creek" seemed natural to the Erwin kids. The girls loved bluegrass's enthusiasm. They cared little that it hardly seemed cool. Besides, their parents loved this unique American music form as well.

Though she played in a youth orchestra and was learning classical music well, Emily not only embraced the fiddle, but by the time she was ten was taking banjo lessons. Soon it appeared she had her eyes set on being the next Barbara Mandrell as she added dobro, mandolin, and any other acoustic instrument she could find. Encouraged by her parents, who not only bought the instruments but paid for the lessons, Emily entered weekend fiddle contests and began to gain notice away from school and home.

Martie didn't sit still, either. Practicing as hard as her younger sister, by the time Martie entered Greenhill High School she was as accomplished a musician as any of her peers; she was just bent in a different musical direction. Her room, too, began to fill with trophies and ribbons for her playing. Though she rarely shared this information with friends, the outgoing teen even dreamed of playing on *Hee Haw*: the much-derided comedy/variety program was one of the few national outlets to showcase the world of bluegrass. In the middle of some really corny jokes, Martie got to see musicians such as Johnny Gimble and Earl Scruggs at their best. Observing the best at work pushed her to practice harder and get better too.

It would have been much easier on their parents if the girls had chosen to simply play in the school band and devote their spare time to the activities embraced by most kids their age—boys, shopping, hanging out at the mall, talking on the telephone, flirting. Yet to Paul and Barbara's credit, they put many of their own interests on hold so their girls could live their dreams. So while the parents of the neighborhood children were racing off to ballgames and cheerleading practice, the Erwins were mapping out ways to get to music gigs that consisted of all-day fiddle contests and hoedowns. Who ever would have thought that those initial Suzuki lessons would lead to putting tens of thousands of miles on a family car while constantly seeking out new venues for bluegrass standards? Before the girls finally left home, the Erwins wore out countless maps of Texas.

By 1984, when Martie was fifteen and Emily twelve, the Erwin girls had earned enough raves at fiddle contests that the word was filtering through music circles about their rare talents and discipline. Pursued by established adult bands, the sisters ultimately joined a teen bluegrass group called Blue Night Express. Thanks in large part to Martie and Emily's skills, the band caught on and soon expanded its appearances beyond Dallas–Fort Worth.

Besides their incredible ability on a wide variety of instruments, the greatest quality that Martie and Emily brought to the group was their blood harmony. Though largely thought of as instrumentally-driven music, good bluegrass can be defined by its vocal blend. With its frantic pacing and unique phrasing, the harmonies can be especially difficult. Yet the way the sisters' voices naturally meshed together, the vocal work of the Blue Night Express soared.

By 1987, the Blue Night Express was well known enough to cross the Lone Star border and travel throughout the Midwest. Appearing mainly at music festivals, the band continued to wow crowds and judges. Often scaling down to just three musicians, the band was dominated by the Erwins. Cute and bright-eyed—though Emily was terrible shy—with their perfect smiles and all-American manners, the sisters won over fans at each new venue. Bookers and festival coordinators liked them too: not only did they play so well, but their youth set them apart from almost every other act on the bluegrass bill. Best of all, they were cheap. Yet for Martie and Emily, their reviews might have been solid, their small corps of fans equally so, and their music fueled by passion, but bluegrass wasn't an end-all. As they grew older, they both were looking ahead at vastly different career options.

After four years chock full of all the normal activities she could crowd into high school between her music appearances, Martie applied for and was accepted to Dallas's Southern Methodist University. At SMU she continued to study music theory, looking to a career as a writer or teacher. Yet even as she took on the challenges of a demanding class schedule of one of the nation's toughest institutions of higher learning, she couldn't let go of her music. Though there appeared to be little future in it, Martie continued to play with her sister in Blue Night Express and to work on improving her playing. In 1987 she even won second place at national Old Time Fiddlers Contest. This was hardly the type of thing an SMU student would normally brag about on a campus that featured many of Dallas's social elite, but it was a satisfying experience for the young woman. She now knew that she was considered good enough to share a stage with the acts she had watched on *Hee Haw*, even if she never had the chance to pick with the likes of Bill Monroe or Earl Scruggs.

With two-hour gigs and long drives to bluegrass concerts and festivals eating her days and nights, Emily was most grateful for understanding teachers at Greenhill High. When she had to miss classes for a gig, they always seemed ready to help her catch up. They seemed to want to do everything they could for this extremely bright student. Emily had told them she was dreaming of going to the Air

Force Academy and someday flying jets—a lofty goal that was at least equal to any challenge she would ever face in the world of music.

Yet even while she dreamed of the Air Force, it was the music that really made Emily fly. She loved the audiences. Like so many who had started playing in front of crowds at a young age, she was hooked on applause. Even though she was shy, she never felt more alive than she did on stage. Giving up football games, cheerleading, dates, and almost everything else to play music seemed worth it. Emily would have performed happily for nothing—and as a bluegrass entertainer she often did. Performing was what mattered most. Watching from the stage as her music connected with someone she had never met drove her to keep working hard and dreaming big.

So while the Erwin girls may have been living in one of the fastest-growing cities in the world, they were continually leaving the bright lights of Dallas for towns so small they didn't appear on the map. In communities such as Overton and Walker, the girls won over old people and farmboys. With their banjo, bass, and fiddles they charmed audiences made up of nameless faces who were satisfied to watch their every move and listen to their unique sound. And though they often might have felt like awkward adolescents, as all teens do from time to time, they never showed it on stage. They were polished beyond their years; daily practice for over two-thirds of their lives had made them skilled musicians. Yet being great in bluegrass didn't mean much at the employment line. In Texas this form of music was often viewed as folk dribble. While hundreds might pull up a lawn chair and happily listen to it on a

Sunday afternoon in the park, few were actually going to pay money for tickets. Bluegrass just wasn't commercial.

For the Erwin sisters, where a large venue was an amusement park such as Silver Dollar City in Branson, it looked like the days of playing for fun were just about over. Nashville wasn't interested in bluegrass, either, and most bookers considered it a musical style out of the pages of history. With Martie in college, facing more difficult academic challenges than she had ever known, and Emily becoming more involved at Greenhill High, their musical instruments might have easily been put away as the girls began to focus on the stuff of real life—the things that mattered to most kids their age. Others might have been benefiting by the doors opened a decade before by Barbara Mandrell and Alabama, but not these sisters—at least not now. Music was fun, it was a nice dream; but it seemed that even a job at the mall would pay a great deal more in the long run.

2

Street-Corner
Singers

By 1989 Martie and Emily Erwin had ridden bluegrass as far as it would take them. The commercial dead end created by the traditional sounds of southern country music seemed to place a huge stumbling block in the Erwin sisters' path to success. And at this point it was even doubtful that success in the music industry was what they really wanted anyway: both seemed ready to turn their efforts to their education and the future it offered. If they did decide to take another stab at entertainment, they might have to start from scratch: their six years in Texas bluegrass weren't likely to provide them with much more than some awards and memories.

But, if a deeper study of the country music charts are any judge, their time in bluegrass was very well spent. Three of the hottest young men in the recent history of country music, Ricky Skaggs, Keith Whitley, and Vince Gill, had all begun their careers as teens performing bluegrass music in the 1970s. Playing the intricate runs and singing the unique harmonies the style demanded provided them with a chance not only to refine their musical skills but to gain the notice of other players as well. The bluegrass experience really did pave the way for Skaggs, Whitley, and Gill to make a move to more mainstream country. If they could do it, why couldn't Martie and Emily?

For experienced bluegrass performers to make a move, they had to be at the peak of their game. Their playing couldn't be just all right; it had to be rock solid. The Erwin girls, who had captured not only the spotlight but a host of trophies in their days in bluegrass, had honed their talents to a point where others had noticed. They were deemed rock-solid musicians by men and women who didn't even like country music. So, in a final judgment, their long-term teenage gig with Blue Night Express really served as the springboard to the next level. Unlike the majority of out-of-work and down-on-their-luck local pickers, these two would soon find themselves in another band.

Like the Erwins, Robin Lynn Macy had begun her musical career very young. She played folk music with her sister during her teens in Missouri, but left the entertainment business when she graduated from high school and headed for college. There, Robin tried to escape the lure of the stage, but even in the midst of studying for history and math finals the spotlight kept calling out to her. Those who knew her well figured she would slide back into some kind of performing once she'd earned her degree, and true to their prediction, after graduation Robin quickly gave up her dreams of public service and a career in law to return to her first love. In 1981 she left the "Show Me" state to show Big D what kind of stuff she was made of.

Macy, an attractive brunette, hit DFW and landed on her feet working in musical theater. Yet the strains of the folk music she had played as a teen meant a great deal more to her than the songs of Rodgers and Hart. She finally gave in to the lure of the small stage and began jamming with some of her new friends. Her talents were quickly recognized by area musicians, so it didn't take very long to get an invitation to join a band. She wasn't about to turn it down.

Four men—Drew Garrett, who played bass; Andy Owens, who plucked the mandolin; James McKinney, a five-string-banjo master; and fiddle player Stephen Dudash—figured that Robin would be the tonic they needed to set their solid bluegrass ensemble apart from the other local bands. With her folk background and guitar abilities, she seemed a perfect choice to transform the male quartet into a mixed quintet. Though she joined the band as just another player, within weeks Robin was its star. She drew the spotlight and the fans.

By 1988 Robin Macy and the band, called Danger in the Air, were on the move. Thanks to her feel for this traditional music, the band accomplished its goal of setting itself apart while earning top-shelf reviews on the bluegrass festival circuit. But, like the Erwins, Robin quickly discovered that while bluegrass might keep you on the run, it didn't necessarily pay the bills. She might have thought of herself as a musician by career, but she paid the rent by teaching math at St. Mark's School for Boys and earned pocket change by giving music lessons. It was teaching that generated the income, but still, she couldn't give the music up. Performing had become a drug; she needed it to feel complete and happy. Without the chance to pick and sing, Robin's life would have had a large vacant space.

She needed to write music as well, and in between her other duties Robin tried to refine her songwriting skills. Rarely satisfied with her finished products, she kept pushing herself to be better. It was this drive that led her to the teenage Erwins.

When Robin Lynn Macy first saw Martie and Emily playing on the bluegrass circuit, it had to have brought back memories of her own high-school years. These kids were living a life that she had lived and were dreaming the same kinds of dreams, too. Yet it was more than just their shared experiences that set the Erwin sisters apart from the other pickers at these acoustic jams; it was also their talent and drive. When she sat down and picked with them, Robin was impressed. She felt at home with them; Martie and Emily might be more than a decade younger than she was but all three were on the same musical page.

For a while Robin must have believed that Danger in the Air would follow the lead of the Whites and become a rare bluegrass band that broke out of the mold and scored in mainstream country. Though the band was very good, it didn't happen. Even a couple of tight and solid self-produced cassettes failed to generate any enthusiasm beyond their small fan base. While other bluegrass groups, like the Texas Rangers, were touring the world, Danger in the Air seemed to be hitting mostly one-stoplight towns.

The band's first album, *Danger in the Air*, was a deceptively good recording: it might have been produced on the cheap, but the picking, arrangements, and harmonies belied the cost. The hand-drawn lightning strike on the album cover could have been a symbol for the recording's electricity and power. Though there were only eight cuts, *Danger in the Air* had a unique feel and proved very satisfying. With songs such as "Bluegrass Show," written by future country star Jodee Messina, the rocking Box Tops' "The Letter," Emmylou Harris's "Sweetheart of the Pines," the very traditionally bluegrass-flavored "Salt Creek," and Creedence Clearwater Revival leader John Fogerty's "Big Train from Memphis," *Danger in the Air* showed stellar bluegrass promise. But except for a few Texas bluegrass fans, consumers weren't buying. Hence, the album was more self-satisfying than anything else. The bottom line probably showed that despite the low production costs, *Danger in the Air* still lost money.

The group's second album, *Airtight*, was another cheaply produced effort that turned out to be a top-shelf product. Though the group had included such great cuts as Bill Monroe's "In the Pines," the Beatles' "I Saw Her Standing There," and the Roseanne Cash hit "My Baby Thinks He's a Train," the release didn't generate any national exposure or major-label recording deals. There would be no third album. Robin was seeing the writing on the wall. Yet her years with Danger in the Air hadn't been wasted. For one thing, *Airtight* contained three of her own tunes, "It Don't Matter," "Storm Out on the Sea," and "Kiss Me Once." Robin now had recorded proof of her songwriting talents — three ready-to-order demos to ship to

Music City's name acts, record producers, and publishing companies.

While Robin, Martie, and Emily were trying to figure out if there was life after bluegrass, Laura Lynch, a thirty-something Dell City, Texas, product, was also spinning her wheels. A divorced mother, the West Texan had grown up on a ranch before heading to Austin to attend the University of Texas. Attractive and bright, blessed with charm and personality that seemed to ooze from her pores, Lynn ended up in El Paso as a local television news reporter. While in West Texas she all but lived the story of many a great country song: she married, had a baby, divorced, then migrated to Houston to start life over again. Trying to get a feel for herself, she signed up for guitar lessons. This led to her attending a bluegrass festival. The moment she first heard the strains of bluegrass classics like "Blue Moon of Kentucky," she was hooked. After honing her picking skills, she spent many nights jamming with friends and listening to bands. On days when she wasn't making a living as a stockbroker or a real-estate developer for the huge firm of Trammell Crow, she was attending bluegrass shows. It was at one of these music shows in the late 1980s that Lynch first ran into Robin Macy. The two immediately hit it off.

Robin was impressed with how quickly Laura had picked up bluegrass. Her bass guitar work was tight and her ability to harmonize was just as impressive. Robin figured it wouldn't take long before Laura Lynch was a force in the Texas bluegrass scene. And she was right: not only did Laura find a spot in the Texas Rangers bluegrass band, it paid well enough for her to quit her day job. Now based in Dallas, Laura played the nation's top folk gigs and even toured Japan. But even though bluegrass was giving her a far more lucrative ride than Robin or the Erwin sisters were getting, the grind of traveling all over the world, and spending so much time away from her daughter, began to make her wish for something closer to home.

In the late spring of 1989, four directionless music-loving souls came together. Though Laura and Robin were more than a decade older than Martie and Emily, the quartet hit it off almost like four sisters. Naturally, they did more than just talk about music; they began jamming together too. Their sound was so solid, their flow so natural, that Robin began dreaming about putting together a band. In her vision, this group wasn't so much a traditional bluegrass ensemble as a new cutting-edge combination of bluegrass, older western music, and new country. In the girls' jam sessions, Robin began to steer the sound in that direction.

With no track record, it would have been next to impossible for an all-girl acoustic group to get a gig in DFW. So rather than audition for a spot in a club or honky-tonk, and certainly not wanting to be pigeonholed by debuting at a bluegrass festival, Robin suggested they play on a city street corner and just see what happened. If the sound didn't come together in this informal setting, then they could all go their separate ways.

This must have sounded like fun to Martie, who was outgoing and more than willing to take a chance on almost any kind of stage. Emily was probably a bit less enthusiastic: her shyness would have made her leery of such close contact with her audience. For Laura, hauling a huge stand-up bass guitar to a downtown Dallas street corner was a large comedown from playing before thousands in Japan. Yet rather than argue with Robin and look for something more traditional, the quartet picked a location and a time. They targeted McKinney Avenue in West End, a section of downtown Dallas famed for its clubs and restaurants, as the place they would premiere their new sound. The date they chose coincided with the start of summer vacation for most schoolkids. It was the time that fit best into the quartet's schedules.

It's hard to imagine setting up and playing unannounced in downtown Dallas. Unlike New York and Chicago, the streets in Texas are not filled with performers working for tips. People seeking money on the streets of DFW are usually homeless or drunk, not actors or musicians between gigs. So for these four attractive women, one of them still in high school, this summer day must have been extremely nerve-racking—probably more so than any bluegrass festival. Surrounded by hundreds of people, all seemingly in a hurry to get to appointments or jobs, and with cars, trucks, and buses blowing exhaust and honking horns just a few yards away, Martie, Emily, Robin, and Laura hit their first note and began singing. When they did, a few of those who had seemed so anxious to rush by them a minute before stopped, turned, and listened. Shades of some Judy Garland–Mickey Rooney movie, within minutes the crowd had grown from a handful to more than a hundred. Suddenly people were smiling, laughing, nodding their heads, and singing along. A few of them were even tossing money into one of the ladies' open guitar cases.

In the first hour they played, the quartet made $375. It didn't take a mathematics professor to explain to the Erwins that their cut for an hour's work would be a great deal more than they could make *at the mall*. Robin and Laura also quickly realized that the change in the case represented more than either of them would earn at an average bluegrass festival. Their shyness gone, the women picked to their heart's content for another hour and then went home happy. Needless to say, they returned the next day.

"We made a three-digit income in about an hour," Martie recalled later in one of their first Nashville press releases from Sony. "[At that point] we all knew there was something magical, or at least lucrative, about women playing music together."

Over the course of the next few weeks, while the quartet didn't generate the kind of cash it had at their debut, people continued to listen and continued to toss tips into the open guitar case. Moreover, the open-air concrete stage offered the women a unique platform. They didn't have to satisfy a booker, they didn't have to worry about judges, and their music didn't have to meet any parameters. They could perform whatever they wanted and whenever they wanted to. There were no sound boards, no lights, and no long nights driving home after distant gigs. It might not have been *Grand Ole Opry*, but it was a lot better than playing in a backwater town for farmers waiting to see whose tractor could pull the heaviest wagonload of corn.

Within a week of the sidewalk debut, a regular fan base

began to turn out to listen. The girls got to know this group and not only took requests, but exchanged small talk as well. The most common question asked was, "Who are you?" After a while, answering with their four names just didn't make any sense. Besides Crosby, Stills, Nash and Young, how many groups simply went by their own names anyway? Erwin, Erwin, Lynch, and Macy sounded more like a law firm than an acoustic band. They were going to have to have a handle to hang their musical hat on.

At first the lack of a name was fun—it was kind of cool to be so mysterious. Yet the girls knew that they would never be booked by anyone off the street if they didn't come up with a moniker. For weeks they each made suggestions; some were all right, others were way out, but none really captured the band's evolving identity. As time passed, and business owners began to ask who booked them and what was their price for a night's work, deciding on a name became essential.

Martie Erwin has told and retold the story of how the group finally got its handle so many times it can be recited verbatim by almost every reporter covering country music. The haphazard manner in which the name was chosen is as much a part of their legend as their music.

"We were on our way to the street corner one day and the Little Feat song 'Dixie Chicken' came on the radio," Martie explained. "That was it! We decided that we were the Dixie Chickens!"

Yet in truth Martie—whose tall, elegant appearance often invited comparisons to movie actress Julia Roberts— didn't really like the thought of being labeled a hen. So after a few days their name was shortened to Dixie Chicks.

It seemed to fit, too: after all, they were playing music in a part of the old Confederate States of America, and they were female.

Not long after they had settled on "Dixie Chicks," the women came up with a logo for their act. The drawing showed a profile of a chicken with long eyelashes. For many of their fans, this image became a symbol of the group and its music. To those who had never come in contact with the band, the logo looked more like a sign at a Chicken Express fast-food joint than a symbol for a musical group.

For a while the Dixie Chicks were satisfied with both the logo and their name. Yet after a few weeks the handle seemed so common that the girls were concerned it didn't have any zing. In an attempt to put a new spin on the name, they changed the spelling of "Chicks" to "Chix." It looked cool. Yet the group soon discovered that the image the four-letter spelling created had very little to do with music. In Dallas "chix" had come to be identified with strip clubs. Some players from the Dallas Cowboys had recently gotten into trouble by frequenting these establishments and hobnobbing with the dancers, and the thought of having themselves pictured as a quartet of strippers convinced the women to go back to the original spelling. They dropped the "Chix," but decided that come hell or high water they were sticking with the Dixie Chicks.

Much more than their unique choice for a stage, the Dixie Chicks were garnering a growing interest because they were not the Forester Sisters or even a female Alabama. They were different. Their music was meshed into something that embraced the rhythm of western swing, the acoustic virtuosity of bluegrass picking, and an almost gospellike "female harmony." Martie explained it this way to a local writer: "It's an acoustic, nostalgic western cowgirl sound. Not that every song has to be 'Happy Trails.' But as a way to categorize it—cowgirl music."

Dale Evans had left Texas decades before the Dixie Chicks had been hatched, but they owed the singing cowgirl and wife of Roy Rogers a great deal more than they did Reba McEntire or the Judds. Dale, along with Patsy Montana, was helping the girls gain an identity. In Texas this style was working because even though Dallas now had an almost midwestern feel, the western heritage was still considered cool. Lawyers wore cowboy boots with their suits, and even transplanted businessmen from Chicago often bought hats. Most had never been in a saddle or visited a working ranch, but they still were cowboys in their dreams. Hence, songs such as "I Want to Be a Cowboy's Sweetheart" made them feel a yearning for barbecue, the smell of a campfire, and a view of a western sunset.

Was this sound commercial? Would it sell better than bluegrass? In Kentucky, no, it probably wouldn't. But as the Chicks began to add western outfits to the street gigs, in Texas the look and sound seemed to fit. It also sold.

Just like the girls knew they had to have a name and develop some kind of unique sound, they also knew they couldn't play street corners forever. Some days it would rain them out; on others the summer sun would drive away their audience. So they had to move on—or in this case, in. As their identity became more defined, as the *Dallas Morning News* even began to write about them, it became obvious they wouldn't have to wait very long to move inside. The people who genuinely liked them and listened to them on the streets were also the patrons of many local clubs and eateries. Seeing a chance to increase their traffic, area business managers began tempting the Dixie Chicks with offers of a real paycheck and air conditioning. It didn't take long for the women to bite.

Off the streets, the ladies soon began playing in restaurants along the West End. As word got out about their showmanship, talent, and special blend of music, the crowds often turned out more to hear the Chicks than to order the chicken or steaks. Almost everyone who heard them seemed to agree they were going to make it big — everyone except those who really mattered.

It would be a while before Nashville took any note of the Dixie Chicks. The women's choice of genre and style seemed to be commercial and cool only on their home turf. This western music might make the group a living in Dallas, but the movers and shakers in Music City didn't see much potential there. Just as the Chicks were moving off the streets and inside for their shows, Suzy Boguss was attempting to carve out a career in country music singing western songs such as "I Want to Be a Cowboy's Sweetheart." While the reviews were good, Suzy's sales were not. And if an act with some recognized status within the circle of country music programmers couldn't make cowgirl music fly, what chance did an unknown group of former bluegrass pickers have?

Alison Krauss had also used some of the sounds and instrumentation now embraced by the Chicks in her Nashville-based music. While the fans at *Grand Ole Opry* loved her and critics raved, Reba was hardly challenged.

When pulling in big money at a concert or on a recording really mattered, Krauss would not be headlining the bill. By most Nashville executives, Alison and Suzy were seen as bit players whose futures were limited at best.

However, as they played for tips and cover charges, it was doubtful that Robin, Laura, Martie, or Emily noticed or cared how Music City viewed acoustic and western music. "We never took ourselves too seriously," Martie recalled later. "Our big aim was to play indoors!"

If this was the case, the Chicks had arrived!

3

Dale Evans's Cowgirls

A t restaurants like Joey Tomato's in Dallas's West End, the Dixie Chicks quickly began charming overflow crowds with their unique style of music. Patrons had to come early just to get into the building. Lines sometimes ran around the block. Overnight the group had become a must-see for the Dallas in crowd.

If one song could fully describe the Chicks' look and sound at this time, it was "Thank Heavens for Dale Evans," a tune written by Martie Erwin and Robin Lynn Macy with help from their friend Lisa Brandenburg. With harmonies that sounded like a mix between the Carter Family of the late 1950s and 1960s, when Mother Maybelle Carter was singing with her daughters, and the original Sons of the Pioneers, the Chicks dressed as if they were the daughters of the Sons. Yet even more radical than their retro-western fringed costumes was the way they used a distinctive bluegrass style on a full range of songs from soul to country to rock. It was as unique and unexpected as Elvis tackling Bill Monroe's classic bluegrass ode "Blue Moon of Kentucky" in 1954 and recording it with a rock-abilly beat on the King's first Sun recordings. Yet for the Dallas crowds who were flocking to see the new female band, the sound worked.

"I Want to Be a Cowboy's Sweetheart" was a classic example of how the Chicks viewed music a great deal differently than anyone else in mainstream circles. "Sweetheart" had been recorded countless times by everyone from its writer, Patsy Montana, to Suzy Boguss, and even by local preteen sensation LeAnn Rimes on one of her independent offerings. No matter the year of the recording, each version stayed true to the completely western feel of the original hit from 1936!

While the Dixie Chicks kept the vocal line and its yodels intact, their instrumental arrangement turned "Sweetheart" from a ballad into a banjo-driven explosion of joy. From the first note it was obvious that the girls who sang this song didn't ride a horse, they took the express train. "Sweetheart" had always been sung a bit uptempo, but the Chicks revved it up even more. In about two minutes the band not only sang all the lyrics twice, but managed to fit in a hot instrument break and a pair of yodeling sessions. It was like riding a roller coaster at a Six Flags amusement park: by the time you got used to the experience, it was over.

When "I Want to Be a Cowboy's Sweetheart" was

played at Joey Tomato's or anywhere else, everyone stopped eating, stared at the stage, and tapped along as the women played. The tapping was good too, because the one element the Chicks didn't feel the need to include in their band was a drummer. Ultimately, this nod to bluegrass tradition was just one of the things that would keep Music City from taking them very seriously. Yet it was a part of the vision that Robin and Laura had for the group: making a statement and creating a personal style was far more important than national commercial success.

In spite of standing against a great deal of musical convention, the Dixie Chicks quickly became Dallas's favorite lounge act. With seemingly weekly mentions in the *Dallas Morning News*, the band went from playing on the streets to being a locally recognized sensation in less than a year. Though they were hardly making big bucks, the quartet was generating enough income and interest to bring both encouragement and a bit of area celebrity. From time to time fans even recognized them at the mall or on the streets. However, even as DFW's "overnight sensations" headed to Dallas's Sumet-Bernet Studios to cut a self-produced independent album, many of those who caught their act wondered if they were anything more than a passing fad. Though they were talented, they were off the wall in such a way that their audience would never seem to grow beyond the local club crowd.

In truth it was only natural to consider the Dixie Chicks the ultimate gimmick group. And it wasn't just the way they dressed. For starters, their sound was like nothing being played on any radio station, no matter what type of music it programmed. What the women played wasn't really bluegrass, but it sure wasn't western or swing, either. There was no doubt it grabbed people's attention on first listen—it was that unusual—but would it wear well?

Their distinctive harmonies harked back to another time: steeped in a bluegrass-gospel tradition, the blends reminded many old-timers of gospel-music families with their own radio programs during the Depression. The Chicks' sound wasn't rich and deep, it was light and airy, but it also had an edge. Most people couldn't even describe it. It was nothing like that of the Sweethearts of the Rodeo or the Mandrell Sisters; it was much more rural.

Yet more than their sound, it was their look that really had people thinking the act shouldn't be taken seriously. The Dixie Chicks' clothing looked as if it had been purchased at a Republic Pictures garage sale in 1947: dresses covered with beads and fringe, western designs flowing from shoulder to shoulder and down the sides. The women often sported cowboy boots that were too short to be cool and not short enough to be considered high heels. With puffed hairstyles that the Andrews Sisters would have adored, the Chicks looked as if they had come in on the latest time machine from the black-and-white days of World War II. Some in the crowd wondered if they had.

The only thing close to the Dixie Chicks in country music was Riders in the Sky. The western trio, made up of Douglas Green, Dr. Paul Chrisman, and Fred LaBour, had started playing traditional western music for fun. Ironically, like all the Dixie Chicks, their first paying gigs were at a bluegrass venue. Adopting the names Ranger Doug, Woody Paul, and Too Slim, and completely outfitted as Rex Allen or Roy Rogers clones, they joked their way to a nostalgic ride that ended with them hosting a program on the Nashville Network in the 1980s. Those who looked at the Riders often laughed at them, but when the trio sang, their clear harmonies evoking memories of the beauty of western music, the laughing stopped. Over time, the group developed a small but loyal following. Yet because they were only perceived as playing to the past, for people who still longed for Saturday matinees at the local theaters, record executives ignored them. So did the major bookers. Riders in the Sky were welcomed on the *Opry* and embraced by many older fans, but they never were taken seriously by Nashville's starmakers. Their niche was simply too small.

To many of those who caught them at their first local dates, the Dixie Chicks seemed to be headed down this same road. While they were seeing an incredible response for the moment, the musical niche they were embracing seemed every bit as confining and limited as the Riders'. Where could they really go in a Dale Evans dress? The ultimate answer seemed to be "not very far."

But amassing more money than they'd ever seen in bluegrass, and watching their small but loyal fan base expand, Martie, Emily, Robin, and Laura didn't care. For the moment it was far better to have people question if they had what it took for the long haul than not to notice them at all.

Playing at Dallas night spots such as Poor David's Pub and Uncle Calvin's Coffeehouse, the band was a sensation. The Chicks liked these gigs because, as Robin put it, "fans come to hear us, not drink or dance." Yet these coffeehouse settings were nothing like the venues where most country acts played. If they wanted to really appeal to mainstream country music fans, they would have to play honky-tonks where people did drink and dance. Would Robin and the women be willing to face crowds who demanded country standards played the way George Jones and Tammy Wynette sang them? While it seemed the Erwins might be willing to expand in that direction, most of those who knew Robin and Laura didn't think they would open up their sound enough to play the dance halls.

They now were calling themselves "the World's Only All Cowgirl Band," and this image really took hold when they released their first album in October of 1990. From the first cut, "The Cowboy Lives Forever," to the last, "Salty," the cowgirl image showed through. Many might have been surprised that there were any new songs on the album at all. Like the women themselves, it seemed to have been born in another time.

At first glance *Thank Heavens for Dale Evans* appeared to be only a tribute to the "Queen of the West." With Dale in a studio shot from the 1940s on the cover, surrounded through computer magic by the four Chicks, shown as if they had been sharing the same studio with her, many who picked up the album must have expected to find classic Evans songs such as "Happy Trails to You" and "Faith, Hope and Charity." Yet what they discovered when they played the CD or tape was the same mix of material that the women had been singing since they moved their act off the streets. It was bluegrass music cowgirl style, and it was much different than anything that had been recorded in at least three or four decades.

A local scribe wrote that the recording was a mix of

"folk music and traditional country with brilliant fiddle performances (including two instrumental cuts) to create a wonderful experience for fans of traditional and contemporary country alike. While the band shines on folk songs like 'Storm Out on the Sea,' their songs with strong western roots (like their cover of 'I Want to Be a Cowboy's Sweetheart') show the most commercial promise."

Commercial or not, the album received its only airplay on local public radio. Not one of the more than a dozen local country outlets considered breaking any of the Chicks' songs. Though it was solid, though it did reflect the group's identity at the time, the album wasn't commercial; it appealed to a very limited public. This stark fact had to have been a disappointment for the women. Yet because their own core of fans liked it, the women weren't going to lose money on the project. In just a few months sales at shows would more than pay back the production costs.

While the most remembered song on *Thank Heavens for Dale Evans* seems to be "I Want to Be a Cowboy's Sweetheart," the simple cut that really stood apart was "Bring It on Home to Me."

In 1962 famed rock singer Sam Cooke had taken his own recording of his song to the top twenty. Three years later the Animals paid tribute to Cooke and put it on the charts again, and in 1968 Eddie Floyd scored another hit with the tune. Then, in 1976, Mickey Gilley hit the top of the country charts with his version of "Bring It on Home to Me." When Cooke penned the number, he probably never guessed that it would cross into so many different genres and appear on the charts years after he himself had died—let alone that a group of self-styled cowgirls would be singing it.

When the Chicks cut the Cooke song, it was trimmed to less than two minutes and recorded without any instrumentation. With no fiddle or banjo behind the vocals, the personality of the Dixie Chicks radically changed. There was a bluesy feel to their harmonies that had nothing to do with cowboys or cowgirls. Though largely unnoticed at the time, when the Chicks finally did hit Music City, a bit of the sound first revealed in the final cut on *Thank Heavens for Dale Evans* would come with them. "Bring It on Home" gave the few thousand Chicks fans who bought that first album a peek into the future.

Though the album was well received in Dallas and the staff at the Sumet-Bernet Studio loved working with the women, the Chicks really didn't enjoy the studio. Unlike live performances, recording was tedious work. There was little freedom to be spontaneous, and every tiny flaw had to be fixed. It was also less and less a group project as it evolved into individuals going over things by themselves, trying to find the right mix to satisfy the other members of the band. Yet more than the simple frustration of the process, it was the stark coldness of the studio that affected the women's attitudes. Like many individuals who loved live performance, the Chicks found the studio offered little feedback. So naturally it was hard for the Dixie Chicks to capture the enthusiasm they felt on stage. This meant that they had to try the same material over and over again.

The women later admitted that there were a lot of tears shed in the almost two-month process of putting together *Thank Heavens for Dale Evans*. Yet at the time the final package seemed to satisfy them all. Because it allowed the hard-core fans to listen to most of the numbers they knew from the Chicks' shows, they liked it too. Though the band had no distributor and no network for sales, the women were able to push enough product at appearances and in local music outlets to average sales of over a thousand copies a month for a year. These were remarkable numbers for a new group with such a radically different sound.

By early 1991, the band had evolved into Dallas's favorite band. Those who considered themselves hip in DFW had to be Dixie Chicks fans. They were the flavor of the moment. But as with certain fashion accessories, few were predicting that the women would remain hot for long. It was a well-known fact that Dallas was a city of fair-weather fans, but as long as the band kept their unique style of dress and music, they probably would continue to sell seats at small local venues. The larger question on many lips was whether there was life for the Chicks outside the DFW area. Were people ready to take them seriously in Houston, Oklahoma City, or San Antonio? It was a question that would have to be answered eventually, but for now the women could make hay while the sun shone on their home turf.

When they weren't performing at small clubs, the Dixie Chicks were picked up to work a seemingly endless line of benefit shows. Within a year of finding a name for their band, the women were the first choice for entertainment at such functions as the Multiple Sclerosis Bachelor/Bachelorette Spectacular, the Dallas Chamber Orchestra fundraiser, and various Dallas Chamber of Commerce events. The women sang *The Star Spangled Banner* countless times before every local sports team's games and provided entertainment for the fans after many of the contests. They even appeared at the Dallas City Hall at Mayor Steve Bartlett's victory reception.

Yet in spite of all the dates that the *Dallas Morning News* society pages covered, to try to expand their fan base, the Chicks also played gigs for almost nothing at community colleges and local high schools. As they quickly found out, being hot on a local level didn't mean constant work or an endless supply of high-dollar jobs.

One of the most important dates the Dixie Chicks hit early in their run was in Telluride, Colorado. When they arrived in the Rocky Mountain State, the women discovered they had been labeled a bluegrass group. Now, explaining the outfits would be a real challenge. Yet in spite of the perception of the Chicks going in, the women wowed judges and fans alike with their unusual sound. In doing so they brought the National Band Championship back to Dallas. With that on their resumé, a few enquiries from Nashville came in; but sadly for the Chicks, there were no offers. With no major label giving them a record deal, Robin continued to teach, Martie didn't quit her music theory classes at SMU, and Laura managed to sell some real estate to pay her bills. Emily, who was now president of the Greenhill High School senior class, had given up on entering the Air Force Academy, but she was still planning on going to college.

Of the four, it was Martie who seemed to have the most problems mixing a career and a real life. Few areas of study are more demanding than music theory. Martie's major demanded that she spend hours not only in class, but at music performances on campus. She also had required labs. She was honest about the stress placed on her when she spoke to the *Dallas Observer*.

"My friends think I have it all—school and the band," Martie explained. "I study as much as they do. I just play with the band instead of watching television." What she didn't say was that beyond school and music, she had no life. She had given up almost everything a college coed holds dear to concentrate on the two areas that she considered most important. In the process she was missing *any kind* of social outlet.

Things were almost as tough on Emily, but the high-school student had an edge: her teachers were more understanding and would work around her absences.

Robin didn't have it easy, either. She had to be in the classroom each day too, teaching her kids. She had papers to grade and lesson plans to make. There were certain times when she couldn't go out of town. If she did play a late weeknight gig, she still had to get out of bed and be her best the next morning. It was not an easy life; yet the money the band was currently pulling in simply wasn't enough to live on.

The summer was the easiest time for everyone. Dates were more plentiful, and the late nights didn't matter. Yet beyond the West End and the social-event niche, the women were still trying to build an audience. When they played an Independence Day show at Fair Park in 1991, only a handful of curious people stopped to listen. Most of the passersby were on their way to see Styx or Cheap Trick and could have cared less about the retro bluegrass-western sound coming from the Chicks' small stage. And in truth, a number of those who did stop and watch were men who didn't care as much about the music as about the marital status of the four beautiful women.

As the year progressed, the dates became more far-flung, but the pay didn't get any better. Still, the women got to see the country from a cheap motor home.

"Our first gig was on a West End street corner a year and a half ago," Laura Lynch told the *Dallas Morning News* late in the year, "Thanksgiving [1991] we played a double concert in Anchorage. Alaskans are crazy about Western swing."

Besides the frozen tundra, their first full year saw the Chicks playing engagements such as the Walnut Valley Music Festival in Kansas, the Louisiana State Fair, and the Big Sam Big Bass Super Derby in the piney woods near Lufkin, Texas. They would tell fans that it didn't make any difference where they played, that these "cowboy sweethearts always have a Lone Star state of mind." While all four must have felt drained from the work and the travel, it must have been far harder on Robin and Laura than it was on the Erwins. Youth, and the lack of real responsibilities that went with being vacationing students during the summer, paved the way for Martie and Emily to have a much easier time with the long days and short nights than did the two older members. This fact was especially true for Laura, who had to be a mother as well as a bread-winner and entertainer. Yet too many good things were happening now to even think about giving up life in the band.

In just over a year the Dixie Chicks had become so much a part of the Texas music scene that they were invited to perform at the Texas Heritage Festival in Washington, D.C. They told their fans, "The DCs got to D.C. to play for George, Babs, and Millie"—the Bushes and their dog. The performances gave the band a chance to perform with another unique Lone Star group, Asleep at the Wheel.

TNN—The Nashville Network—also put out an invite, and the group enjoyed the exposure on the country music cable giant. Due in no small part to a combination of their look and their sound, more and more people were talking about the Chicks. Even if they didn't have a record deal, word was getting out, and fan clubs were even being formed.

Because of their "happy sounds and smiles," there did seem to be something infectious about their performances and their music. Laura Lynch told a local reporter it was the joy that their music brought to people that had allowed them to rise from the streets so quickly. "If it makes us happy singing it," she explained, "then we figure the fans will enjoy it too."

Critics and fans began to compare the women's harmonies with the Everly Brothers', the Gatlins', and the McGuire Sisters'. Yet even though the Erwins did have the blood relationship, the Chicks' sound and blend were much different from those of any of these former hot acts. If anything, they sounded more like the blend created when Dolly Parton, Linda Ronstadt, and Emmylou Harris performed together. Still, the songs the women chose often didn't allow them to really probe deeply into the haunting potential of their harmonies.

When Garrison Keillor brought his Prairie Home

Companion radio show to Dallas, he invited the Dixie
Chicks to join him. As the local NPR affiliates had already
plugged their *Thank Heavens for Dale Evans* album, the Keillor /Chicks union seemed a natural, and so it was. Keillor's
fans loved the nostalgic rural feel of the Dixie Chicks' performance.

Riders in the Sky reached out to their sisters in fringe
as well. The cowboy singers had their own radio show, and
they happily featured the Dixie Chicks a few times. The
special group who loved the Riders naturally liked the
Chicks.

The quirky CBS television drama *Northern Exposure*
noted the Chicks and used some of their music as background. Though the series' ratings weren't the highest, the
millions who tuned in had to count for something. Every
shot at a national audience, no matter how small, was a
blessing, but what Keillor, Riders in the Sky, and *Northern
Exposure* offered were mere drops in the bucket compared
to McDonald's signing the women to sing a jingle for the
hamburger chain. "You deserve a break today"—well, this
was one. Yet the players in Music City either missed all
the exposure or weren't impressed. No matter how many
calls they made or how many letters and demos the Chicks
sent, record executives simply wouldn't give them the time
of day.

Realizing that their devotion to the pure sounds of
bluegrass and western music might be holding them back,
the women not only expanded their group by a member to
update their sound, but also gave up their ID as an "All
Cowgirl Band." By adding Tom Van Schaik, a college-
trained drummer, to their mix, the Chicks made a conces-

sion to earn wider notice and show they were serious about making it in mainstream country music. The move must have worked, too. Buddy Lee Attractions, one of Music City's largest and oldest bookers, offered to take the women on as clients. It was a move that stunned most in Nashville. Lee had never before signed a band that didn't have a manager or a recording label; many believed he was putting the cart before the horse. But Buddy had seen the women play and thought they could make money on a national level. He also was convinced that a major label would soon step forward and make the women an offer.

In 1990 they had been playing on street corners for tips. Sixteen months later Laura and Robin were able to quit their jobs and give themselves completely to their music careers; the group had sold almost twelve thousand copies of their independent album; they had a respected booker, had recorded a commercial jingle heard all over the country, and were beginning to draw raves from industry insiders as well. "I think the Dixie Chicks are great," bluegrass lover Emmylou Harris told the media when asked to comment on what new groups were ready to storm country music. The traditional country music performer added, "Their music is good and refreshing; I think it would be wonderful to hear them on the radio."

"They make people happy, they're so pretty and so good," observed Ed Bernet, owner of Sumet-Bernet Studios. Bernet, who had helped the women obtain some of their first bookings, added, "If they weren't pretty they'd still be good, but being young, pretty, and talented is an unbeatable combination."

"They're already more than a local success," Steve

Harmon, a local country disc jockey, told the *Dallas Observer*. "They fill all the houses they play. What they're doing is so different, it's not mainstream anything. It's fun to watch. But for national success, they'll need a couple of lucky breaks and a couple of lucky songs."

"I think we're carving our own niche," Robin told a reporter as she looked back over the first eighteen months of work. "We don't really want to conform to formula country music. We want to do what we feel in our hearts."

The problem seemed to be that Nashville wasn't interested in their hearts; they wanted a formula that would put money in the cash register. Adding a drummer was a start, but because the Dixie Chicks wouldn't conform completely, Music City wasn't going to risk much money or time on them. The labels wanted to have the power to mold their artists, not wait for them to find themselves.

Still, even without an interest from the record labels, the fans in Dallas thought the women were headed for the big time. John Anders, a writer for the *Dallas Morning News*, observed that the locals had better catch them now at small venues: he predicted that in the near future the Dixie Chicks would be playing in the country's largest.

Yet with their fringe outfits, cowgirl hats, boots, and bright red lipstick, the women still seemed like a novelty act to those who caught them for the first time. If the songbirds were taking themselves seriously, it was hard to see. If they were joking, then the joke would probably grow old very soon. That would have been a shame, too, for as Anders observed in his review of one of the Chicks' 1991 performances, "There is, to be sure, something truly unexpected about them. They sing, they shine, they play like crazy."

The Nest
Loses a Chick

A s if caught in a time rift, one member of the group wanting to look back, the others desiring to taste the potential they saw in the future, as a gift for their local DFW fans the Dixie Chicks ended 1991 by releasing a special Christmas package. *Home on the Radar Range* was recorded in Dallas and issued as a 45 rpm single. On one side was "Christmas Swing," and if you could find a record player and adapter to fit the record's large hole, the other side would play "The Flip Side." Sold with a photo jacket sleeve that featured the four Chicks dressed and made up more like housewives from an episode of *The Donna Reed Show* than country music performers, the entertaining Christmas disc was another example of the band's struggle for an identity. As the fans listened to the only real record the band would ever produce, they had to be asking if their favorite songbirds were going to devote themselves to embracing the past and be satisfied being considered a novelty act or were going to drop the pigeonholing trappings that painted them as nothing more than a female version of Riders in the Sky.

This question of identity and direction had to be answered quickly. The Chicks had booked time in the studio to cut another album early in 1992. While *Thank Heavens for Dale Evans* had managed to sell over twelve thousand copies in a year, it had also failed to generate the kind of industry enthusiasm needed to gain radio play or land the band a major-label contract. In truth, the women hadn't even had a label show any interest in them at all. So before their next effort was recorded, the band had to determine if they were going to make a break with the image that had seemingly overnight made them Dallas's hottest ticket or take off in a new direction and transform their act into one that could and would be accepted by mainstream country fans everywhere. As it turned out, rather than address their growing dilemma, the band came to a compromise that would leave them spinning their wheels.

Most music critics now believe that the Dixie Chicks probably would have moved easily toward the musical center if not for Robin Lynn Macy. Since childhood Robin had embraced the roots and strains of folk music. It was her background and tastes that had been the principal vision for the creation of the Chicks. She really didn't care as much for what Nashville wanted or the country radio stations played as she did about keeping her vision of the group and the sound pure and untarnished by commercialism. Her individualist streak ran deep, and she didn't want to sell out even if it meant losing a chance for fame and fortune.

For several months the members of the group had each been quietly lobbying for what they wanted for the band. Over time push had begun to come to shove. By early 1992 it had also become obvious at the concerts that Robin was not controlling the band as she had in the past. Laura Lynch was taking a more up-front role, and her voice was being featured on more of the group's numbers. Though fans saw no discontent or any hints of the creative battles that were being fought, a major conflict was developing that would determine not only the future direction of the Dixie Chicks' music, but even their membership.

When the band walked into the Sumet-Bernet Studios in the winter of 1992 they were not a united group. There were two different viewpoints as to what sound the project needed. The team approach that had begun on the sidewalks of Dallas was now beginning to die. Because so much was riding on each song and each career move, the split was being exposed quickly and causing a lot of deep pain and hurt feelings.

In the end the 1992 recording session would clearly signal that the girls were no longer satisfied being a Dallas novelty act. As the tracks were laid down, at least two-thirds of the sound that came through the monitors and across the mixing boards was much different than what had been captured on *Thank Heavens for Dale Evans*. While the choices being made would not be radical enough to alienate their hardcore fans, they would deepen the musical chasm that was growing between Robin and the other Chicks.

The tension in the studio was obvious not only to engineer Larry Seyer, but to almost anyone who came by. Even members of the local press picked up on it and reported that the month of recording work had taken a heavy toll on the band. The *Dallas Observer*, seemingly unaware of the creative differences between the women, indicated that the work on the album had driven Robin Lynn Macy to tears on several occasions. While most blamed stress, those on the inside knew Macy's emotional outbursts were due to heartbreak too.

As the fourteen tracks for the new album were laid down, Robin must have felt as if she were losing a child. The outfits, the music, and the performance style that had made the Dixie Chicks so hot so quickly had been her idea. She had been convinced this type of female band not only could make money, but would also be preserving an important part of American music's past. Now, just as her dream was beginning to prove her right and fly, the other members of the band were flying to a much different tune.

Robin, who had been such a dominant force on the first album, now had been reduced to just another player. She was given the lead vocal on only six of the cuts. Much worse than that, her influence was dying as well. It seemed that Laura Lynch was now the team leader.

As the *Observer* correctly noted, "because *Little Ol' Cowgirl* is the vehicle the Chicks' hopes ride on, expectations are high. So much depends on this record. The women struggle to keep their goal in sight as they labor over the many little choices that will lead to success—or won't." In Robin's mind, what the other women wanted was all wrong. To her, it must have been like denying her faith.

As she played on the more mainstream country cuts, she must have been hit with the realization she was starting to abandon the music she loved.

The other Chicks were worried too. They had a great deal to gain—or to lose. The departure from the cowgirl/bluegrass sound was enough of a break that even the Erwins and Laura wondered if the fans would like it. Having drums on every track might turn off some of those who had drifted over from a background in pure bluegrass music. That was what Robin believed. Yet the fact was, there just wasn't much money in bluegrass or traditional folk, and even less future. Laura, Martie, and Emily no longer wanted to be the big fish in a pond called Dallas; they dreamed of swimming in the same waters as Garth Brooks and Vince Gill.

As the Chicks put the finishing touches on their second album and wondered about its effect on their futures, a host of famous fans were embracing them. At the White House, George Bush mentioned he liked their music and had them play at a couple of fundraisers. So did one of his rivals, Ross Perot. To round out the presidential sweepstakes, Arkansas native and country music lover Bill Clinton cast his swing vote for the Dixie Chicks too. It was about the only thing that all three men could agree on. The women refused to take sides; the band would happily play for anyone—Democrat, Republican, or Independent—who gave them a stage. By March, the tripartisan love affair with the band had been noted by the *Washington Post*. (Having received an advance copy of *Little Ol' Cowgirl*, Michael Corcoran wrote, "The sound quality is exceptional. The Chicks' trademark harmonies are equally pristine.")

Having a Dixie Chicks fan in the White House seemed a sure bet, but the question remained whether their new album would have the same effect on the capital of the music world—Nashville. If it didn't, then the risk they were taking with this new sound might not have been worth it.

The March 1, 1993, issue of *Dallas Life Magazine*, a Sunday addition to the *Dallas Morning News*, prefaced a long feature story on the band by asking the question "Can the Dixie Chicks make it in the big time?"

Freelancer Renee Clark's story began, "Since their first performance in 1989 on a West End street corner, the Dixie Chicks have had both stunning success and an equally stunning lack of it."

In one sentence Clark had completely summed up the band's history. She had also fully defined both sides of the group's personality. If all they wanted to be was the DFW group who won the *Observer*'s annual fan choice award as the "favorite local band," then they were an unqualified success. Yet if they wanted to spin off and gain acceptance by mainstream country music, then they had failed. But was that local success keeping them from achieving the other, larger goal? Three of the members seemed to believe it was, and even Robin Lynn Macy might have agreed; but being just a hot Dallas act didn't seem to bother her as much as it did her more ambitious colleagues.

In a very real sense, the Dixie Chicks themselves, like the *Dallas Morning News* and the *Fort Worth Star-Telegram*, had to wonder why Music City had not asked the band to join the "big dance." In terms of independent releases, *Thank Heavens for Dale Evans* had been a huge success. Their

McDonald's jingle was giving them national exposure, along with clips of their work being shown on TNN and CBS's popular newsmagazine *60 Minutes*. The Chicks had a drawerful of great performance reviews. Besides, for more than a decade artists like George Strait had proven that Texas music could be hot everywhere. An industry rule of thumb had long been that if an artist played well in the Lone Star State, then America would love that artist's work. So why hadn't the Dixie Chicks been picked up by an industry that thrived on finding the latest fad and cashing in on it?

The media and the band knew the ultimate answer to that question might come as early as April, when *Little Ol' Cowgirl* was released. Would it take them closer to their big dream? For the band, the waiting was hard.

When Ms. Clark interviewed the band's members for her story, Robin Lynn Macy seemed to be the most uneasy with the Chicks' growing urge to be noticed by Nashville. Robin downplayed the need for the new project to open any doors at all. She told the reporter, "I think we're carving our own niche. We don't really want to conform to formula country music. We want to do what we feel in our hearts. Whether that will translate to super-stardom, I kind of doubt it. But I think as long as we're making enough money, and we're happy playing the music, who could ask for more?"

At about the same time, KPLX-FM disc jockey Steve Harmon noted, "They're already more than a local success. They fill all the houses they play. What they're doing is so different, it's not mainstream anything. It's fun to watch. But for national success, they'll need a couple of lucky breaks and a couple of lucky songs." This less-than-ringing endorsement from the area's leading country station must have hurt the girls a bit. If they made it, they wanted it to be on talent, not luck. What Harmon probably meant was that the women were going to have to find the right formula to fit the Music City mold while still keeping a sound that would set them apart from the sixty or so other major recording artists fighting for a place on the national playlists.

Though clearly meant as a transitional project, with its picture of a four-year-old girl dressed like a miniature Dale Evans *Little Ol' Cowgirl* still sold the same old image on the album jacket. Yet under the skin it was at least a semi-different sound. It revealed a group that was evolving beyond a novelty act. While the instruments were still mainly acoustic, the sound now owed more to Emmylou Harris and Dolly Parton than it did to Dale Evans and Patsy Montana—though you wouldn't realize this if all you listened to was the first two cuts.

The title cut, "Little Ol' Cowgirl," was very much a bow to the group's past. If the remainder of the album had stayed in this western vein, then Robin's long-term vision for the group would have probably remained intact.

The second track, "A Road Is Just a Road," was again a blend of folk and cowboy music. Robin had the lead vocal again. With its straightforward bluegrass arrangement, this Mary Chapin Carpenter–penned number would have easily fit the Chicks' first album too.

It was the third cut where the group's transformation became clearer. "She'll Find Better Things to Do" was driven by Laura's hot lead vocal, with the other three ladies harmonizing on the chorus. From beginning to end it was modern country, a song that could have been cut by Faith Hill or Reba McEntire. A local radio station aimed at the high-school and college crowd even picked it up and put it on their playlist. There were rumors that only Robin's protest kept the women from investing their own money and shipping the single to all the nation's major country outlets.

"She'll Find Better Things to Do" did more than just provide a map of the Chicks' new direction. The women brought the steel-guitar wizard Lloyd Maines to fill out the music on this track. Maines's work on the session not only brought an electric instrument to the band's mix, but served to introduce his daughter, Natalie, to the Dixie Chicks' music.

As revolutionary as "She'll Find Better Things to Do" was, "Irish Medley," which followed, was nothing more than a trio of traditional folk ballads that had little in common with anything being played by country radio. It would have fit in much better at an O'Donnell family reunion than a country music concert. This cut was anything but commercial.

Continuing an interest they showed on their first album, the Chicks then added another Sam Cooke song to their package. "You Send Me," the best-known work by the rock-and-roll star, was given a unique bluegrass twist and uptempo ending—and as strange as that may sound on paper, in the studio it worked like a charm.

"Just a Bit Like Me" showcased Robin's songwriting and voice. Looked at now, the song's lyrics seem to give an insight into the creative war being fought at this time. "If we could do it all over, would we still be satisfied?"

was one of the cut's more haunting lines. For Robin the answer was probably no. Yet the song itself revealed the artist's talent for both composition and strong vocal interpretation.

Like "She'll Find Better Things to Do," "A Heart That Can" seemed ripe for the current country radio playlists. It was good, but hardly great. While the arrangement was entertaining, it didn't set the band apart from many others trying to land a deal in Nashville.

"Past the Point of Rescue" was simply the band's cover of a recent Hal Ketchum release, while the next cut, an instrumental, "Beatin' Around the Bush," was a bow to the picking talents of the Erwin sisters. Both cuts were nicely done and appealed to the group's fans.

"Two of a Kind," the album's tenth pick, again featured Laura's lead vocals. It was solid, but not spectacular.

"Standin' by the Bedside" may have been one of the women's most interesting choices. In a Stamps-Baxter "shaped note" tradition, Lynch's vocals hark back to the sound of the original, legendary Carter family recording of "Can the Circle Be Unbroken." This marked the first time the Chicks had recorded a true gospel song, and it served to reveal how close their harmonies were to those long heard in small southern churches.

Robin received a "peace offering" when she recorded "Aunt Mattie's Quilt," a folksong that could have probably found a place on an early Peter, Paul and Mary album. Yet her voice was in far better form on the next cut, the Ray Charles blues hit "Hallelujah, I Love Him So."

"Pink Toenails" rounded out the album while also foreshadowing a move that had to be made in the future. The song would become a Dixie Chicks standard and crowd favorite a few years down the road when Natalie Maines joined the group and performed the lead vocal. Laura Lynch's work on this song does not have the gut-level drive that Maines brought to the number when she joined the Erwin sisters.

In spite of its seemingly split personality, a host of Texas critics predicted that *Little Ol' Cowgirl* would be the album to drive the group to a major label in Nashville. Even in retrospect, it seemed to indicate a band ready for the big time. Yet Music City must have sensed that the women had not fully meshed and evolved enough to be ready for the national spotlight. The often diametrically opposed musical styles and choices that had found their way onto *Little Ol' Cowgirl* indicated that the creative war for the Chicks' identity was still undecided. So those who made the big deals in Tennessee were going to wait and see what happened over the course of time.

Though Nashville was still taking a pass, the Dixie Chicks were moving well out of Texas and playing dates across most of the mid-South. They also continued to find unique ways to gain attention.

The June 28, 1992, edition of the syndicated newspaper feature *Ripley's Believe It or Not!* contained the following little known facts.

In 1991, 2,000 builders in Cascais, Portugal, erected a 64-ft. tower made out of 250,000 LEGO Blocks!

Jeff Myers of Phoenix, Ariz., has invented a Square Ball that bounces like a round one!

The Dixie Chicks, a Dallas, Texas based country band, uses a Double Bass Guitar shaped like a Large Cactus!

As the women found themselves in the world of *Believe It or Not!*, they had to be wondering when country music would simply believe in them. Yet with or without the backing of a national record label, they were selling albums and now pulling down as much as $2,500 a performance. For the Erwins and Laura Lynch, playing the road was a pretty nice way to make a living. Meanwhile, Robin Macy was wrestling with her own professional goals and desires, and money had little to do with either.

With their fan base growing, the Chicks put together a mailing list and began to issue newsletters on a semi-irregular basis. Called *Chick Chat*, the mailings were often filled with nonsensical observations of life on the road, as well as future booking information and a marketplace page for their products. In the summer of 1992, the rambling letter spoke of Scrabble, fast food, and getting lost in Oklahoma. The band wrote of seeing the world at seventy miles an hour, tightly packed into an oversized van and longing for homecooked meals. They also mentioned that Bryce's Cafeteria in Texarkana had the best coconut cream pie in the world.

The merchandise hawked in *Chick Chat* included both the Chicks' albums, their 45-rpm Christmas release, T-shirts, bags, bonnets, and pictures. The growing selection of products listed on the final page of their newsletter and filling their autograph tables at shows — and the fact that scores of fans not only bought those items, but stayed late to have their pictures taken with the women — indicated the band was connecting with mainstream country crowds. Their growing checkbook balances signaled the same thing.

Still, there can be little argument that the Chicks' healthier appearance fee had been driven up as much by having Buddy Lee as their booker as it had by their growing success at shows and in the studio. Lee, a trusted industry icon for decades, had gotten the word out that the women were crowd pleasers and that venues that took a chance on them would not be disappointed. So while the band was still playing places around their home base like Fatso's in Arlington, Texas, private parties for business such as the Texas Comerica in Fort Worth, and smalltown shows like the Spring Creek Festival in Garland, Texas, they were now getting some bigger dates as well.

On July 4, 1992, they came back to the State Fairgrounds in Dallas. A year before, the band had drawn only a handful of (mainly male) admirers. Now they were playing on a stage sponsored by a beer distributor, and this time the crowds had grown. So had the enthusiasm for their performance. Like the crowds at their other recent shows, this one seemed to really like their more mainstream country sound.

Two weeks later, on July 17, the Chicks played at Nashville's Station Inn. Music City loved the band, and many fans stayed late to visit with the four women. Country star Suzy Boguss was one of those who chatted with these country music wannabes. Though no one knew it then, this turned out to be the final time the original Dixie Chicks appeared in Tennessee together. The next time Boguss caught them, they looked a great deal different.

Two weeks after the Nashville show, as the band performed a five-day package for the Fiesta Texas amusement park in San Antonio, the creative differences that had been pulling the group in vastly different musical directions finally split them up.

The process that had begun during work on *Little Ol' Cowgirl* had continued when, on an earlier break in their touring schedule, Robin Lynn Macy had spent a few days at the Kerrville Folk Festival. When she left for the trip, Robin had told the three other women she needed to go and work on her songwriting. What she probably was doing was seeking out her own musical roots and trying to decide how far she had strayed from them. In the small community of Kerrville, Texas, as she listened to and played the fundamental acoustic music that had first driven her to perform as a teenager, she probably realized she didn't have much use or any passion for mainstream, 1990s country. There can be little doubt that as she rejoined the Dixie Chicks, she had to have known her days as a member were numbered.

Two days after the last Fiesta Texas performance, Robin announced she was leaving the band that had once been like a child to her. She wrote to her fans in *Chick Chat*, "It is time to move on and take a road less travelled. So, to all my friends, thanks for the many memories. And for now, I bid a fond farewell."

Few could have blamed Macy for staying true to her vision. She was a woman of conviction and passion. She had to believe in what she was doing and where she was going. If she had stayed with the Dixie Chicks, she would have been forced to "fake it"—something she could no longer do.

Though the Erwins and Lynch valued Macy's friendship, they also knew it was time for a split. They understood why she was going. Yet they felt just as strongly and passionately about the direction they were taking and what they needed to do.

After saying goodbye, they replaced Robin with guitar player Matthew Benjamin and didn't miss a beat. Now the band had just three-part harmony, and Laura became the only lead singer. A week after the breakup, the trio of Chicks played in Austin, then boarded an airplane and hit California for a three-day appearance at the Mid-State Fair. This new version of the Dixie Chicks was not only as solid as ever, but also much more focused on meeting the expectations of mainstream country audiences.

In mid-August the band returned to Nashville and worked on the TNN series *American Music Shop*. Nashville's most respected fiddle player, Mark O'Conner, performed with the Chicks. It especially thrilled Martie to play with a fiddle master, and the appearance seemed to be another sign that Music City was beginning to recognize that the band had some commercial appeal.

Robert Adels of *Cash Box* magazine was certainly impressed. After catching them on their West Coast debut he wrote, "The Dixie Chicks come across as the most exciting female threesome since Dolly Parton joined Emmylou Harris and Linda Ronstadt for the *Trio* album."

Adels's review, found in the heart of one of the music industry's most important publications, should have created some new interest in Nashville. Yet if any of the Music City movers and shakers noticed, they didn't let the Chicks know it. Maybe the powers at the labels were simply waiting to see how the band would evolve without the talented Macy.

The three remaining members were now completely focused on making it as a modern country act, and the Dale Evans trappings were slowly being phased out, but the Chicks still had to face the boredom and trials of life on the road. The mechanical breakdowns, the money spent on food and lodging, the lack of sleep, and the constant pressures of making the next date were just as debilitating and draining. To stave off boredom the group would play scores of games of Scrabble, count the peanuts in boxes of Cracker Jacks, and read the tabloids. Lost in a whirl of one-night stands and long hours in the van, they lost track of television, the news, and even the passing of the seasons.

As the incredibly hectic and eventful year finally began to wind down, the Chicks performed at a Dallas Cowboys halftime show, the New Mexico and Texas state fairs, and countless smaller venues before ever growing numbers of fans. Yet in the second issue of *Chick Chat* they indicated that while the dates were becoming bigger and better, the money was not adding up like it should. The women figured that by the time they finished paying for their booker, the hired help, the makeup and costumes, the cost of travel, food, and hotels for themselves and their band and their lighting and sound men, they were not making as much as they did in Dallas playing on the streets.

The moaning about money was simply another Chick joke. But the women had discovered that becoming more successful in the public's eye did not always translate into success measured by the music industry. A lot of acts had risen to the point where the Chicks were now, only to die on the vine when they didn't get a record gig or failed to sustain their creative drive. While the three women were worn out from a long year of work, and looking forward to spending Christmastime with family and friends, they knew they had a great deal more work to do in 1993 if they expected to make it where it mattered: in Nashville and on country radio stations—two places a female country band had never found any lasting success.

5

Three Chicks
Crossing the Road

The Dixie Chicks began the year with a bang, by packing their bags and heading back to Washington, D.C. This time they were booked to play at newly elected Bill Clinton's Presidential Inaugural Gala. They probably would have been invited for the big night if Ross Perot or George Bush had won as well. Sporting their big hair and western outfits, they charmed the audience, but as they would admit in their own fan club newsletter, they were charmed as well.

"The Inauguration was all it was cracked up to be: beautiful, festive, real big and snazzy. We were proud to be the Texas Ambassadors—yahoo! Better yet, we were honored to be bumping rhinestones with many of our musical heroes 'n' heroines like Emmylou Harris, who looked like the angel she is, and Kathy Mattea — she blew the walls down with a killer performance as usual."

The women took advantage of their time at the gala, Martie getting to visit with Paul Simon, Laura sharing conversation with the likes of Jimmy Buffett, who didn't have a clue as to who the Dixie Chicks were, and finally sharing a stage with Jerry Jeff Walker. It was a big night for the band, and they were awed to be in the rarified company that surrounded them. As they wowed the nation's elite, they must have felt as if they were walking on air. Yet while they were visiting the city that thrived on strife and conflict, they were about to find some of their own. Making the move to a more mainstream country sound would turn into a battle, and there would be more casualties.

Looking at their first full year without Robin Lynn Macy, the Dixie Chicks were now openly courting the Nashville power brokers. The band's three women were very straightforward in their attempts to catch the attention of anyone who had a nationally distributed record label. Whenever they were given a chance, they talked openly with the press and fans about their desire to move up the music ladder to the big time. But while Buddy Lee Attractions had lined up a long list of shows for them to play, the record thing just wasn't happening. In spite of their frank and direct approach, as well as the small but loyal base of fans they already had in their corner, they couldn't attract a serious interview with even a small national label. As all three women were both talented and good-looking, there had to be some other reasons Music City was not acknowledging them.

At least a part of this lack of interest had to do with

the fact that female bands were an *unknown* commodity in country music. Women groups just weren't taken seriously. The most common comments made about women who had formed all-female ensembles in the past had been "Aren't they cute!"

Well, the Chicks were cute, but they were also solid musicians. They had done their homework, and each member had racked up a decade of professional performances. Still, while Nashville was perfectly willing to take a chance on Billy Ray Cyrus or Faith Hill, an unknown group of women from Texas seemed to scare the music industry. The Dixie Chicks were generating the same kind of apprehension that male country bands had before RCA had finally taken a chance on Alabama.

Much more than the fact that the Chicks were blazing new trails with a female band (and especially now that their drummer and guitar player were men), what seemed to put record labels off the most was that they couldn't put their finger on exactly what the Dixie Chicks were. Were they bluegrass, western, a novelty group, or a folk trio? Whatever they were, it was as unclear in 1993 as it had been on the streets of the Dallas West End a few years before. They genuinely seemed to have no real direction.

With the Erwins now out of school and Robin Lynn Macy out of the band, the Chicks did have more freedom of expression and time to practice and to tour. They also had a pink motor home that could take them almost anywhere—when it was running—so their willingness to hit the highway had to play in their favor. Record labels usually wanted their acts to perform at least two hundred shows annually, in as many different parts of the United

States as possible. Yet even that age-old rule of "Sell your-self first on the road" was about to change. Shania Twain proved a performer could make millions before even con-sidering hitting the circuit.

In truth, the Chicks' willingness to tour the nation was considered by many to be as strange as their past choices of recording material. It was rare for country music artists who didn't have a record deal to be traveling across the States, appearing in cities thousands of miles from their home base. With nothing to sell, it would have seemed to benefit the women to stay home and cut their expenses. Yet during 1993, complete with their spangles and rhine-stones, the Chicks could be seen in almost every state in the Union. The money they were pulling in—big dollars for a local band—was only enough to keep them going on the road. As Music City veterans knew well, the expenses of trying to go national ate up most of the cash flow. So despite traveling tens of thousands of miles each month, the Chicks were still stuck in a rut. They weren't bringing in much more money, and weren't getting any closer to landing a record contract.

The thing that most held the group back was the image that had first caused them to be a sensation in Dallas: Dale Evans costumes. People simply had problems taking them seriously. They were fun, enthusiastic, and off-the-wall, but no one seemed to see much substance beneath the fringe and spangles. None of the powers behind the labels were looking for a female version of Riders in the Sky.

Another thing that got in the way of the Chicks being looked at with much respect was their name. In the days of women's liberation and equal rights for the sexes, "chick" didn't seem politically correct—it wasn't a term embraced by the kind of thinking women the band wanted to attract.

Without realizing it at the time, by making a name for themselves as the Dixie Chicks the women had backed themselves into a corner. Their small but loyal following knew them only as the Dixie Chicks. So it just didn't make much sense to become "the band formerly known as the Dixie Chicks." Yet, as a number of public relations experts informed them, the name itself just might be the stumbling block that kept them from becoming any more than they already were.

Stuck with a name many women and record executives didn't like, the band tried to give the term "chick" a new meaning. They began to talk about Chick Power: a trio of women empowering themselves to accomplish everything within their potential. Any man who tried to get in the way of the confident women—confident and assured enough to embrace the term "chick"—would be run over when these chicks decided it was time to cross the road.

And that, essentially, was what the band really needed to do: cross the road to mainstream country music. If the talented trio could play the kind of music that was being heard on the radio and somehow manage to hang on to a bit of the sound that set them apart from everyone else in Nashville, then their name, their gender, and their image would not keep them from landing a recording contract. However, the ifs always seemed to be working against them.

The feedback they were now getting from sources in Nashville was that their second album had been much too scattered, with cuts that ranged from folk to bluegrass to mainstream to gospel to old rock-and-roll. To a record scout the Chicks appeared ungrounded; they needed some kind of center to draw from. Once again the term "identity" came into play. Even though *Little Ol' Cowgirl* was selling well at their concerts, it seemed imperative to book more studio time and try for a product that would finally define them as ready for a chance at the big time.

The big time, however, was a much harder-to-reach destination than it had been in the past. In old Nashville, artists had been given years to develop by a label. Legendary performers such as Patsy Cline and Mel Tillis had toiled for more than six years before ever hitting their stride. During this period the record labels had loyally stood by their budding stars. They had shown faith in them and patiently waited for the artists to grow and produce. Even as recently as fifteen years ago, when Reba McEntire had struggled to find her stride, her label had been willing to go along until the singer grew up as an artist. Now it was a different ball game.

Modern Nashville was a lot like baseball—three strikes and you were out. If artists didn't score with their first couple of releases, they were shelved. Not only did their label drop them; it often seemed that the entire industry turned its back on them as well. The reason for this lack of nurturing was money.

When Barbara Mandrell had landed her network television show and brought a wider spotlight to country music, a good-selling album by a big artist might hit 100,000 units in total sales. Alabama then came along, opened doors for new fans with a lot of disposable income, and the world changed dramatically. By the early 1990s, a star was expected to average at least 500,000 units with every new release. With more money on the line, more money was being invested in acts too. Keeping an unsuccessful artist on board would now cost the labels six-figure losses — money that could be better used developing new acts. There was no time to be charitable.

In most Music City minds, the Dixie Chicks had already swung at two pitches and missed badly. Neither *Thank Heavens for Dale Evans* nor *Little Ol' Cowgirl* had inspired much confidence from the record labels. If anyone was ever going to take the huge gamble of signing a female-driven band, then that company was going to have to be given something up front that showed some real across-the-board commercial appeal. The label had to be sure that the chances for success were at least even, if not stacked in their favor.

As Laura, Martie, and Emily were now all on the same musical page, the fight over what direction to take the band had ended. Yet even as they continued to draw packed houses in the Dallas area and nice crowds of several hundred to a couple of thousand around the country, they also understood they didn't have much time left to find the right formula for success.

When their gigs were reviewed, the clippings were almost always identical. Critics first wrote of the women's incredible talent. The scribes were almost universally amazed by the Erwin sisters' artistry on guitar, dobro, fiddle, and banjo. The reviews then usually spoke of the women's "Frederick's of Cheyenne" outfits and seamless harmonies. By and large, most critics were wowed by the potential they saw and questioned why no major label had signed them.

While almost everyone saw the group's talent, a few also picked up on the things about the Chicks that most frightened the labels. When the group sang original material, it wasn't groundbreaking or even very strong: the Chicks simply couldn't generate the same excitement with their own stuff as they could covering other artists' hits. One writer even went so far as to call them nothing more than a band trying hard to make it to *Star Search*. The remark was probably intended as the ultimate slam; but the Chicks were well aware, even if the critic was not, that Sawyer Brown had gotten their big break in country music on the very same TV series.

Opening for Kenny Rogers in Branson, Missouri, at the huge Grand Palace Theater was a good gig and great paycheck for the Chicks. The audience who attended the series of shows appreciated the women too. They liked the band's bluegrass/western feel and applauded politely after each number. Yet, as most of those who had bought tickets to the Rogers show were retired and rarely purchased any music by new country artists, even this response didn't mean much in Music City. In Nashville the scores of theaters that lined the streets of Branson were viewed as retirement homes for out-of-work former stars. It was a city where people came to see past heroes, not listen to today's hot stars.

At about the same time the Chicks played the Grand Palace, a writer caught their performance before 250 people in another small venue. He chimed in with this less-than-enthusiastic view of the same basic show the women had used in the Ozarks:

> The Chicks could get by on great covers, so engaging is their musicianship, but they don't seem to reach much further than the obvious when choosing which songs to reprise. "Leavin' Louisiana in the Broad Daylight," sung exactly as Emmylou Harris did it, is the sort of thing you'd expect from a cover band with bills to pay. Also, the heavily harmonized, slowed-down version of Sam Cooke's "Bring It on Home to Me" was a curious choice . . . it smacked of a Vegas lounge routine. On that number, the Dixie Chicks tested positive for Branson—they certainly had the non-stop smiles to succeed in that Missouri monument to schlock.

Yet there were still many small venues that booked the band over and over again. In places like Rockefeller's in Houston, Texas, capacity crowds of several hundred came back every time the women played. Not only did these fans like the women's choice of material, but they enjoyed the fact the Dixie Chicks were simply a fun group. They took their music seriously, but not themselves. During a time when almost every major performer was claiming to have the answers to everything from gun control to who should be the next President of the United States, the Chicks simply played music without dispensing dogma. For paying patrons their show was refreshingly easy to take and offered a wonderful way to escape the real world. Yet it was that same real-world audience the Chicks were going to have to impress in order to broaden their base of support and land a record deal.

Expanding their influence meant doing whatever was needed to get exposure. At one point they even drove all the way to New York and played in front of the Ed Sullivan Theater all day long, just hoping to gain some attention from the man who hosted a network show there, David Letterman. It didn't work. In fact they were asked to leave, but not before making enough money to pay for an expensive New York hotel room.

Over the course of their coast-to-coast travels they met and rubbed elbows with real stars such as Liza Minnelli and Bob Newhart and were greeted with bizarre looks by others thanks to their unique wardrobes. It was a learning experience, to say the least.

A local bootmaker, Justin of Fort Worth, Texas, decided the women were the perfect models for its product. The women negotiated a deal where they received free boots if they posed for a poster. Soon, even though few outside the DFW area still really knew who they were, the Dixie Chicks were on shoestore walls from California to Florida and Texas to Canada. They traveled so many miles that their original blue van died, so they replaced it with a pink motor home.

Ralph Emery and TNN called them from time to time, and they always jumped. Yet most of their appearances were in places like Abbotstown, Pennsylvania; Hereford, Texas; and Paso Robles, California. They still needed a highly detailed map to find many of the small venues that booked them.

At about the same time as their appearances with NPR network star Garrison Keillor, the original Dixie Chicks had made a number of visits to local programs broadcast over the public radio outlet in Dallas, KERA, during which the band had usually performed. Some of these performances were packaged by KERA into its *Sound Sessions* CD release. The Dixie Chicks music featured on the recording was pure bluegrass. Though the album was not widely distributed and received little press coverage, the fact that the Chicks again sounded like a cult band rather than a mainstream country wannabe meant that *Sound Sessions* couldn't have been issued at a worse time. What buyers of the special album heard was a long way from the direction that Lynch and the Erwins wanted to go.

About two-thirds of the way through a very demanding year, the Chicks headed back to the studio to tackle recording their third independent album. They went in knowing that this very well might be their last chance to impress the powers in Music City. This time the final package had to be the result of a team working together, not individuals picking and choosing what they wanted to play and what sound they thought was right. There was no question, the Dixie Chicks' future depended on agreeing on each number and each arrangement.

The ladies felt that showing the major labels that the Dixie Chicks were willing to use their sound and style commercially was the only way Nashville would understand that the band had market potential and that the women would listen to reason and accept change in their music and their wardrobe. They needed this album to be a platform to display their growth as musicians and maturity as a group. Realizing what was at stake, the women decided to produce the project by themselves. Whether the album flew or crashed, it would be because of the choices they'd made.

Those who had watched the Chicks fight and cry their way through the 1992 album and simply work and laugh their way through the earlier *Dale Evans* were immediately impressed by the different manner in which the women attacked this project. These Chicks weren't emotional or flighty, but organized, deliberate, and focused. Like a clutch hitter stepping to the plate in the ninth inning of a World Series game, they had done their homework and were ready for the challenge in front of them. If they struck out, they were going to go down swinging.

When the *Dallas Morning News* asked Emily how their approach to this album differed from their other two trips to the studio, the new high-school graduate was refreshingly direct and honest. "I think this time we had a lot more time to sit down and figure out what we wanted to put on this album."

Her sister then chimed in: "We had a lot of guidance. We're very open, and don't have a problem with an idea that isn't ours. That's part of growing—you can't always call the shots, which is what we've been doing since day one. Sometimes you've got to take people's advice, let the pros go in there and do what they want."

Martie's carefully worded and thoughtful statement was probably aimed more at the executives at the major labels than to hometown readers. She wanted RCA, Sony, and all the others to know the Dixie Chicks could listen to advice and change to meet the market's expectations. Like Reba McEntire, the Chicks considered themselves strong and capable women, but also like the Oklahoma redhead, they'd listen and work with anyone who invested in their future.

This time they didn't return to the Dallas studio that had been the home of their first projects. The Chicks hit the road and traveled to Nashville, paying for studio time and using many of the same musicians who worked with the big labels. Crystal Clear Sound did a great job moving the production techniques up a notch. Yet it would take more than good sidemen and a top-rate recording studio to make this effort stand head and shoulders above their past work. It would take a new sound as well.

It seemed to the Chicks that going to Music City to record paid off. Several weeks and countless hours spent in the studio produced an album that was much different than the first two releases. Even the cover was a radical departure: though the three chicks were still dressed in western-style garb, it wasn't in the style of Dale Evans — they were three modern women outfitted to make music, not to play cowgirl. Yet that photo only hinted at the major changes to be found on the tracks inside the CD or cassette.

From the fiddle lick that launched the initial cut, *Shouldn't A Told You That* contrasted greatly from *Thank Heavens for Dale Evans* and *Little Ol' Cowgirl*. "Whistles and Bells" was three minutes of two-steppin' honky-tonk that could have been plucked from a vintage Ray Price or Mel

Tillis album. The electric guitar and steel guitars were out front and obvious. This arrangement was a long way from bluegrass and a radical departure from the Chicks' past work. Though honky-tonk music was not very commercial in 1993, the sound first displayed on "Whistles and Bells" was still fresh and welcome. Best of all, it captured some of the energy the Chicks always had on stage but had largely failed to generate in the studio before now.

"I'm Falling Again," the second-place hitter, was an up-tempo ballad again embracing a honky-tonk feel. The chorus's close-knit harmonies were much like those used early in Emmylou Harris's country career, but the song itself had an up-to-the-moment commercial feel. The cut (written by the Chicks and their first male guitarist, Matthew Benjamin) presented the women not only as a band that understood what was happening in country music, but as writers who could match this understanding with their own compositions.

The title tune came up next. "Shouldn't A Told You That" had a modern bluegrass feel to it, the kind of sound that Dolly Parton often wrote into her material. Laura's vocals were cute, direct, and made even stronger by the Erwins' blood harmonies. The song was infectious, driven by topflight guitar and fiddle music, highlighting lead licks that Ricky Skaggs or Vince Gill would have loved to tackle. "Shouldn't A Told You That" was ultimately electric bluegrass (even if the instruments used were purely acoustic — the kind of song Brenda Lee might have sung in her heyday as a rocker.

"Desire" really gave Laura a chance to present her voice as a strong and inflective force. Again the ballad proved that the band had the ability to give itself fully to mainstream country while keeping their rural harmonies and incredible picking intact. If possible, the musical riffs on this number soared even higher than Laura's lead vocals. By now it was obvious that there had been no war for a direction in the studio. This album was the result of a team of players united in vision and goals.

"There Goes My Dream" finished up the first half of the album on really a down note, sounding more like an Everly Brothers B-side than a first-rate standard. Laura Lynch's vocals didn't lift "Dream" out of its sleepwalking pace. It's about a minute too long, and not a vehicle for the group's stronger qualities; while it was the weakest song on the album, it still reflected a sound that could be at home in a modern marketplace.

"One Heart Away" sounded like a Reba McEntire cut. Co-written by the Chicks' drummer, Tom Van Schaik, the song again didn't seem to have the energy found in the band's live shows. It might have been better with a highly overdubbed, full-blown Nashville ballad treatment rather than the simple and honest approach chosen here. In the past this would have been a welcome sound bite for the retro Chicks, but in the face of the album's first four songs, "One Heart Away" was second-rate.

"The Thrill Is in the Chase" was probably included because it had been penned by Lynch. Not especially melodic or catchy, it might have played better with a different arrangement and a gutsier vocal. Yet even this downturn was an upbeat answer to critics who had seen the band as only a novelty or retro set.

"I Wasn't Looking for You" not only presented a great

opportunity for the "New Chicks" to strut their stuff, but allowed an unsung Chick to fly solo for the first time. Martie Erwin took center mike, and her voice, though not as strong as either Robin's or Laura's, had a sincerity that made up for what it lacked in power and range. Written by Matthew Benjamin, "I Wasn't Looking for You" was a beautiful, plaintive ballad that might have been a hit for Emmylou Harris in the early 1980s. A haunting cut filled with wonderful lyrics, it displayed for the first time that the Erwins didn't need to lurk in the vocal background.

"I've Only Got Myself to Blame" had a chorus that rang with incredible three-part harmonies. There was a touch of bluegrass in it, the kind that Ricky Skaggs or the Whites would have used; but the arrangement—largely a product of Martie Erwin's talents—had pulled the old country sound into the modern age. With its solid vocal blend, rapid but easy pacing, and wonderful picking, it made a great live concert piece.

"Planet of Love" caught Laura Lynch at her best. She took a number that might have once been considered a big-band torch song and reshaped it into a blues ditty. Slow, unhurried, and very intimate, it has a live feel that seemed to draw the listener into the session. The music flew out of the stereo and lingered in the air, like Reba McEntire's old hit, "Sunday Kind of Love." "Planet of Love," though not at all meant for country radio play, was a wonderful way to cap a project that displayed just how far the Chicks had come since their number had been trimmed to three.

If the Dixie Chicks had hoped to generate radio play with a few of the cuts on "Shouldn't A Told You That," they would be disappointed. If they had expected all of their old fans to like their new sound, they would have likewise been let down. Radio didn't pick up the independent offerings, and many of their fans thought they had sold out their look and sound. Yet the album was being studied in Nashville. The new sound was also beginning to bring mainstream country music fans to their concerts. They had proven that they could adapt their traditional sound to create something unique and commercial.

The Dixie Chicks premiered *Shouldn't A Told You That* with a concert at Dallas's historic Granada Theatre on November 11, 1993. The local fans bought up the fifteen dollar tickets and ate up the menu of new sound. It was gratifying; but the women knew the audience they had recorded the album for would not be in the seats of the old theater, but in offices in Tennessee. What would they think when they heard it in Nashville?

In their newsletter the Chicks wrote, "It's our third album! We oughta be gettin' it down right." They were aware that they *had* to get it right, too.

In another of a seemingly endless string of interviews with the newspaper that had all but become a fan rag for the trio, the *Dallas Morning News* broached the subject of how long the band would stay together if they didn't land a major label contract with this outing. Rather than duck the question, Martie faced it head on. "We fully expect to hit that fifteen–twenty-year mark. But we plan to stay in Texas. I think it's inevitable, when you play country music, that you have to deal with some of those Nashville things. Nashville has a lot to offer, and their support can do a lot of things for us, but right now Texas is where our fan base is, and that's what makes this thing work."

Yet as the *Morning News* and the *Dallas Observer* hailed them again as the best local band, it seemed obvious that all three of the Dixie Chicks wanted more than hometown stardom. Instead of playing a schedule that included performing with the Fort Worth Ballet (the dancers wore western garb), singing *The Star Spangled Banner* before more local sporting events, and being signed up for another year of fundraisers for local charities, the Dixie Chicks yearned for bigger things. They wanted to retire their pink motor home, jump on a custom touring bus, and open for a major country act. However, Martie's answer on the importance of making it in Nashville seemed to indicate the women were beginning to have strong doubts about it ever happening.

The person who had to be suffering the most was Laura. As she labored hard and long to make her own musical dreams come true, her daughter was growing up without her. Asia, who was now thirteen, needed her mother at times when Mom just couldn't be there because Mom was a Dixie Chick. For Laura Lynch, *Shouldn't A Told You That* seemed like the last shot. If this didn't move the Chicks up the ladder, then the group's veteran vocalist probably couldn't hang on much longer. The struggle between being a mother and being a Chick was beginning to cause her a lot of heartache.

For the Erwins, who were still quite young and had a lifetime of adventures to look forward to, the fact that many news articles and critics were still saying "Who are the Dixie Chicks?" was not as pressing a problem. Yet both of them realized that if the pressures of the road and lack of national recognition caused Laura to burn out and leave them, it would be awfully hard for the Chicks to continue as a viable force, even in Dallas. Odds were, Martie and Emily would have to begin again with a new group of people. If that happened, all they had invested in the Dixie Chicks would then just be memories.

The air of uncertainty that had clouded much of 1992 had continued through 1993. Even with the strong new album and their hometown still claiming them as the best band in the land, it appeared the Dixie Chicks were no closer to getting the big break needed to push them up a level. They were much closer to a breakup that might destroy the minor success they had had.

If Music City was going to call, it had to be soon.

6

Chicks on Tour But Going Nowhere

There was a great deal to hope for in the New Year. The new Chicks album, *Shouldn't A Told You That*, was finding some serious play behind the doors of a number of Nashville record labels. Country music was taking some note of Dallas's best-loved band. Yet even as their third album began to force people to take a second and third look at the commercial potential of the Chicks' music, the current market seemed to be working against them.

More often than not, the Dixie Chicks were classified in a very small area of country music now reserved for the Sweethearts of the Rodeo, the Forester Sisters, Wild Rose, and the Whites. Some member of the press included the Mandrell Sisters in this group, but because Barbara, Louise, and Irlene had never had or sought any kind of joint record deal, nor had they ever charted with a group record, the Mandrells couldn't accurately be lumped in with the others.

The Sweethearts of the Rodeo were not technically a group, either, but a duo made up of two sisters, Janis and Kristine Oliver. They had gotten a shot at recording by winning a national talent contest in 1985. Beginning in 1986, the sisters charted ten times for Columbia. Their peak playlist position had been number 4 in their first year of work. Their last two singles, "If I Never See Midnight Again" and "This Heart," in 1989, had hit number 39 and 25 respectively. Columbia had dropped the act from their label soon after that, and the Sweethearts had been on the downward cycle ever since.

The Forester Sisters were a quartet of real sisters from Lookout Mountain, Georgia, who had gained a great deal of national exposure after being signed by Warner Bros. and opening for Larry Gatlin and the Gatlin Brothers Band. Not a band but a vocal ensemble, Kathy, June, Kim, and Christy were much more closely related to the Gatlins in style and substance than to a country music band such as Alabama or Diamond Rio. From 1985 through 1987 the Foresters racked up five number-one hits. They continued to chart through 1991, but then the bottom dropped out and Warners quit pushing them.

Wild Rose really was a female country music band. Pamela Gadd sang the lead vocals, Wanda Vick played guitar, Pam Perry plucked the mandolin, Kathy Mass the bass, and Nancy Prout pounded the drums. Strong musicians with a number of inside-the-industry connections, Wild Rose was pushed as the first women to really do it all, on stage and in the studio. They were a real band. Yet even with a great deal of exposure and publicity, Wild Rose charted only twice and never had a single in the top ten.

Finally, the Chicks were often lumped with Whites because of both groups' bluegrass roots. The Whites were not an all-female band, but a family ensemble. They had been playing together since 1971, with Buck, the father, joining his daughters Sharon and Cheryl on stage. Two other family members once played bluegrass festivals with the group, but retired from show business before the group was hired by Elektra/Curb in 1982. Over the course of the next four years the Whites would chart a dozen times, but never really score a major hit. Their best-selling entry was "Hangin' Around," which hit number 9 in 1983. Though still popular with the bluegrass crowd and the *Opry* fans, the group seemed to prove to Music City that there was no future in trying to market bluegrass-based music.

Still considered by many to be a bluegrass band despite their recent attempts to shed that image, the Chicks had to know that in the history of country music only one pure bluegrass record had ever hit number one. Ricky Skaggs had taken a Bill Monroe classic, "Uncle Pen," and pushed it to the top of the charts in 1984. For a span of more than a year the studios became enamored of the acoustic sound; thus they had signed groups like the Whites. But within two years that enthusiasm had died, and even Skaggs's brand of modern bluegrass was being dismissed by the fans as merely a fad.

As bad as women's groups and bluegrass had fared recently on the charts, females in general were in almost as dire straits. Reba McEntire, who had ruled country music in the mid-1980s, had only one number-one song in 1990, 1991, and 1992. In 1993 she hit the top of the playlists only with a Linda Davis duet, "Does He Love You." Women as a whole were not selling even like they had a few years before.

In 1990 five different women hit number one. The next year only two solo female efforts could top the charts. In 1992 there were four number-one songs by women, but by only two artists, Reba and Wynonna Judd. By 1993 the number was three chart toppers, one of which was the McEntire/Davis duet, which had been pushed by an incredibly inventive video.

With women and bands seemingly on the slide and bluegrass not even in the picture, it seemed that the Dixie Chicks might have made their move to a mainstream sound a little too late. They had a lot of hurdles to cross to land a contract now. They also had to pray that some women in Nashville would begin to make some impact on the charts as well.

As Laura, Martie, and Emily faced another long year of touring, with shows that would take them across the Atlantic and to Europe, in the face of a dismal market for women they had to take heart in the fact their fan base was growing. A great deal of that had to do with the explosion of the World Wide Web. Several sites devoted to the Dixie Chicks had sprung up, but one Dallas-based destination stood out above all the others.

Robert Brooks had been following the Chicks almost since their inception. He had taken his information to the Web early, and his incredible site documented a great deal of the women's work. Those who had even a passing interest in the women were given a Cook's tour of the Dixie Chicks' history just by clicking onto Brooks's page. Amazingly, unlike many other Web sites that would appear just a few years later, Robert's was not as much about fan worship as it was a straightforward, honest documentation of the sound and style that made the women unique. Complete with album reviews and reprinted features, this Internet site probably had a great deal to do with not only spreading the news of the group's talent to new fans, but even generating interest among Nashville labels. Amassing hits from all over the world, Brooks was somewhat of a prophet and unpaid public-relations agent. He and his site (www.dallas.net/~totoro/dixiechicks) will never earn much acclaim for the good work they did on the women's behalf, but their impact, as well as the other news found on the Internet, helped keep the band's name in front of a segment of society hungry for almost any kind of information. Though there are now scores of sites devoted solely to the Chicks, Brooks's is still one of the most interesting Web sites centering on one subject on the whole of the WWW.

Being pushed on the Net was one of the newest ways to gain notice, yet the best and oldest way of being introduced to new fans was touring. This would be the year the Chicks literally drove the wheels off one van and put tens of thousands of miles on another. They would work almost whenever and wherever they were asked. This road work, along with the new album, should have at least gotten them some auditions at a few labels. Yet it didn't.

As hard as they tried, mainstream country just didn't

With her high energy level, Natalie was ready for the crowd in any situation. She was already a cheerleader as a freshman in 1990. *(Seth Poppel Yearbook Archives)*

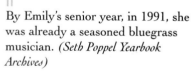

By Emily's senior year, in 1991, she was already a seasoned bluegrass musician. *(Seth Poppel Yearbook Archives)*

Martie was ready for a career as a professional singer, but at this time in 1988 it appeared she would be headed down a classical road. *(Seth Poppel Yearbook Archives)*

In 1998, a year away from the national spotlight, the Dixie Chicks were about to leave Texas and head to Music City. *(© Vicki Houston)*

The original flavor with Laura Lynch in the middle, 1994. The Chicks would soon push Macy out of the nest and add Natalie Maines to the mix. (© *Vicki Houston*)

By February 1998, the trio was on its way to the top, playing at a small club in Wichita Falls, Texas. (© *Vicki Houston*)

Always fan favorites, the Chicks often spent hours signing autographs and posing for pictures. At a benefit for the West Texas Rehab Center in 1998, the trio was already riding the wave of national recognition. (© *Vicki Houston*)

The stars of the 34th Academy of Country Music Awards show in Los Angeles on May 5, 1999, pose with their three awards. (*Paul Fenton*)

The Chicks with Chicks wannabe Boy George, celebrating their American Music Awards win in January 1999.
(© *Ron Wolfson*)

The Erwin Sisters and Natalie Maines share a group hug with one of Music City's other hot sister acts, the Kinleys. *(© 1998 Ron Wolfson)*

Vince Gill, whose background was also bluegrass music, got the Chicks one of their biggest early breaks by booking them as the band for his charity golf tournament. He remains one of their biggest backers in the music industry. This reunion took place in February 1999, just before the Chicks won three Grammys for *Wide Open Spaces*. *(© Ron Wolfson)*

Even out of the stage outfits, the Chicks has one of the hottest looks and acts in the music business. *(© 1998 Ron Wolfson)*

Martie, Natalie, and Emily arrive in style at the American
Music Awards, in January 1999. They took home one of the
highly coveted honors that evening. (© *Gregg Deguire*)

seem to be impressed with anything they did. When they played *Grand Ole Opry* or visited with Lorianne and Charlie on *Crook and Chase*, the record labels always appeared to be looking in another direction, both literally and figuratively. By and large the evolving band was still being viewed as less cutting-edge and much more retrospective. To most of those who make the big Music City decisions, the Chicks were still simply a female Riders in the Sky.

Early in the year, the Texas trio, who hadn't yodeled on a record in some time, flew to the Swiss Alps (among other stops) to try their hand at entertaining people who didn't know much about country music or Garth Brooks and by and large didn't speak English. Dolled up in their cowgirl finest, for two weeks the Dixie Chicks won over fans throughout Europe. Yet the incredible response in Zurich and Brussels didn't seem to mean much in Nashville. For all the good it did them, the Chicks might as well have been on a vacation rather than singing their hearts out. Yet they were now much too focused on making it big in Music City to give up. Always appearing positive and sure, they pushed on across America when they returned to the States.

Over the course of the year the Dixie Chicks would play almost anywhere. The women lived a paraphrase of the old biblical verse: wherever one or two people were gathered, there the Chicks were in the midst of them. On the spur of the moment they would take out their instruments in hotel lobbies, on trains, on big-city streets, or even on airplanes. Wherever they played, they won new converts. Most who saw them vowed to catch them again and told others about the incredible trio of women. So even in the face of fatigue and the feelings of being unappreciated by the music establishment, the Chicks found hope. This hope must have been a strong motivating factor as the year moved slowly on.

The pressures of being on more than two hundred dates a year would have brought most normal men and women to their knees. Yet Laura, Martie, and Emily seemed to not only enjoy the demands, but thrive on them. The harder it got, the more they seemed intent on crossing that road to prosperity and fame. In good times and bad they joked about almost everything. At concerts they would announce their latest album had just won a major honor: it had gone aluminum. To them it meant that they had sold 10,000 copies and were making money. Humor was one way of surviving when the movers and shakers ignored everything they had to offer.

At places like Nile Cowboy's Revue in Billings, Montana, and Billy Bob's Night Club in Fort Worth, the women played in smoky barrooms to crowds who danced more than they listened. It was something none of them really wanted to do, and gigs Robin Lynn Macy probably would have turned down. But if the Chicks were going to go mainstream country, then they had to play honky-tonks. That was just part of living up to Nashville's expectations of paying your dues.

When they weren't in bars, they performed at some the strange gigs where country bands had ever been booked. They played music at junior highs and Christmas parades. They worked benefits and birthday parties. They played for private functions at fancy hotels like the Hyatt and entertained conventioneers in civic auditoriums such as the one in Lubbock, Texas. Poor David's Pub in Dallas used them when they were in town, and IBM had them come to Virginia for a company shindig. In the meantime they were heralded by the likes of George W. Bush, the future governor of Texas and presidential candidate, country legend Merle Haggard and baseball great Nolan Ryan as one of the best bands in the land. Yet true as that was, their DFW fans could have caught them for free at least three times during the year.

Every once in a while, the women would come home musically to their roots. At places like the Winfield Bluegrass Festival they would play the songs they cut their teeth on and relive the simple days of shows on courthouse lawns and getting to bed before the sun came up. Yet while they enjoyed going back to their musical home for a visit, none of the three was interested in staying there forever. A taste of the past just made them want to become big stars even more.

In Somerville, Massachusetts, just outside of Boston, the women were booked at Johnny D's. The crowd, many of whom had never heard the strains of real Texas music played by real Texans, went nuts. The Chicks had to wonder, if they could play country music successfully in both New England and Texas, winning new fans everywhere they performed, then why couldn't the labels understand that they could thrive as mainstream artists in modern country music? Yet wondering didn't do them much good. The Chicks had to let the press do the wondering, and keep themselves focused on the positives.

Back in Dallas, Robin Lynn Macy had resurfaced with a new trio. She had joined two friends to again play traditional country/folk music. Her Domestic Science Club was now beginning to fill some of the same places the Dixie Chicks had once occupied. The new group was slowly catching on in DFW. Yet though Robin would find some satisfaction playing the music she loved, Domestic Science would never challenge the Dixie Chicks in style, substance, or popularity; nor would the group ever be seriously courted by the country music establishment.

As the long summer of working day after day wound down, the Dixie Chicks could only look forward to an equally grueling fall. Yet what was most amazing was that in the mix of a year that seemed to be stealing every spare moment the women had, each of the band members was somehow finding time to have a social life too.

Very quietly Martie had been seeing a young businessman. Though it was not common knowledge among her fans, she was planning to get married.

Emily, who was just a year past worrying about a prom date, was dating Heath Wright of the country band Ricochet. Ricochet had something the Chicks wanted, a record deal. Yet Wright couldn't seem to get the band's label, Columbia, interested in the Chicks. By the end of the year, he'd also lost out in landing Emily.

Meanwhile, Laura wasn't as much worried about dating as she was concerned about the many special moments she was *not* spending with her daughter, Asia. These time-consuming tours had taken the mother away from her child even more than in the past. For Lynch this separation had to be a living hell. If she had been able to give her daughter a higher standard of life through her work, then it might have been worth it. But in truth, Lynch probably could have done much better financially in the hot Dallas real-estate market than she could playing country music in some of the places the Dixie Chicks had been booked. Yet, somehow fueled by the addictive dream of entertainment, she pushed on and prayed her hard work would pay off before her daughter was grown.

In the fall the Chicks were alerted to the fact that they had made the front page of the *New York Times*. The women's exhilaration quickly turned to disappointment when they saw the photo. The newspaper had been doing a story on Ross Perot. The picture that was used had been taken when the Dixie Chicks performed at one of Perot's functions. The newspaper caption didn't identify them, only Ross, so once again millions were asking, "Who are they?"

At another big social gig, President Bill Clinton showed up to watch the Chicks. Later in the evening he and Laura danced. At the time the Chicks would have been happy just to have been mentioned in a potential scandal. They needed press coverage of almost any kind. Yet no one took a photo. It was one of the few times the Washington media missed an opportunity to catch Bill Clinton with a beautiful woman in his arms. While it was also a missed opportunity for national coverage for the Chicks, at least Kenneth Starr didn't call Laura to be grilled by a grand jury.

CBS This Morning finally put the Chicks in the spotlight. Paula Zahn not only interviewed the women, but asked them to play in the studio. The bad news was that while doing the show was fun, the program was rated so far below *Good Morning America* and *The Today Show* that only a handful of sleepy-eyed people probably saw them. The good news was at least Zahn had gotten their name right!

Yet maybe the biggest deal that happened during this time was being booked to play for one of Bruce Willis and Demi Moore's Planet Hollywood openings. Though the spotlights dwelled more on the big-name guests who showed up to christen the club than it did on the band, the Dixie Chicks had to be pleased to be rubbing elbows with stars like Tom Arnold and Roseanne.

Though it might have been hard for the Dixie Chicks to really understand why Nashville still wasn't calling, the number of Music City stars who were pushing for the band to get a gig in the city was growing each month. Former bluegrass musician Vince Gill was not just singing their praises whenever he had the chance, he even booked them to play at the party for his charity golf tournament. This gig exposed the women to other stars, like Amy Grant and Garth Brooks, and a host of record executives as well. For many of those who made the final decisions on the big deals for the name labels, it was the first time they had been able to put faces on the band. Even if it wasn't readily apparent at this time, this exposure, made possible by another star who had once starved for recognition himself, had to have done some good.

At the West Fest the Chicks not only got to play their new music, but performed with the likes of other cowboys such as Red Steagall, Waddie Mitchell, Don Edwards, Michael Martin Murphey, Collin Raye, and Amado Pena. So while they were still playing at a lot of very simple and unheralded gigs — such as appearing with longtime Dallas children's TV host Mr. Peppermint on his local early-morning program — by and large it was obvious the Chicks were moving up, if only very slowly.

A six-week western tour rounded out the year. The trek included a week-long stay at Arizona Charlie's Las Vegas Casino. The Dixie Chicks Vegas premier was in a gambling establishment that bragged not about its show-girls and high-stakes games, but about its bingo and bowl-ing alleys. Arizona Charlie's was definitely not the big time, but at least it was in a city that never sleeps. The crowds that stopped off between trips to the lanes and the games seemed to like the Texas cowgirls as well. Still, except for the week in Vegas, all the western tour really offered the women was playing backwater towns to crowds who had never heard of them. For the tired road warriors, it had to be disheartening.

The Dallas media had predicted that this would be the year the world discovered the Chicks. While the women traveled the world over, their shot at fame seemed no closer than it had in 1991, 1992, or 1993. Country music still didn't seem to be ready for them.

On radio stations the hits were being churned out by the likes of Faith Hill, who scored two number-one songs with "Wild One" and "Piece of My Heart," Trisha Year-wood, who broke in for two weeks with "XXX's and OOO's," and Mary Chapin Carpenter, who lasted only a single week at the top with "Shut Up and Kiss Me." No other women ruled the charts at all. The only bands to manage any time at number one were Shenandoah, with "If Bubba Can Dance, I Can Too," and Little Texas, with "My Love." Country music was now almost exclusively a solo or duet male hat game. The moneymakers were Brooks and Dunn, Vince Gill, Alan Jackson, Clint Black, Tim McGraw, and a handful of others. Women and bands were once again just background players. So the forecast for landing a record deal looked worse now than it had at any time since Robin Lynn Macy left the group.

Had the Dixie Chicks wasted a year working like the devil only to still be considered the best band in Texas not to have a record deal? Was it really worth the effort to continue to struggle and not be given a chance? These were hard questions that didn't have easy answers. At this moment, with one member planning a marriage and wondering if she would want to begin that union by leaving home for long months on the road, and another member of the threesome becoming more and more distraught about the time she was spending away from her daughter, the Chicks' future looked very unsure. Many wondered if the songbirds were about to land in Dallas and stay there for good.

7

New Chicks in Town

Over the holiday break and before the Dixie Chicks hit the road in 1995, Emily was stopped by a Dallas policeman for an illegal U-turn. Using a longstanding country music tradition, she attempted to "bribe" the officer by offering him a copy of the band's albums. The cop turned her down flat: he didn't need to accept the tempting gift because he already had all three. Besides, Emily had to learn that taking a U-turn could get a person nowhere but in trouble.

The ticket story would become symbolic of the Dixie Chicks' coming year. Change was in the wind—not the kind of change that would lead the band to Nashville, but the kind of change that would begin with the pain of separation and the heartache of misunderstanding. Could the band, which already seemed fragile, endure another breakup?

Even though she planned on being married soon and was busy picking out a dress and silver patterns, Martie remained committed to the band. She assured everyone that she would give up a honeymoon and the life of a new-lywed to tour two hundred or more days in the year. Emily, whose own romance with Heath Wright of the country band Ricochet had gone south, was firmly grounded in the concept of giving everything she had to the Chicks. That seemed to leave only Laura not sold on the fact that touring more would mean a better chance of getting a deal in Mu-sic City. The Chicks' lead singer really wanted to cut back on the heavy touring schedule.

Being with her daughter for the holidays probably heightened the anxiety Laura had been feeling for the past few years. She didn't like being an absentee mother. She wanted to spend more time with Asia and less time playing music in nameless clubs in towns that she had forgotten almost as soon as the Chicks' RV pulled past the city limits. Besides, giving more time to touring didn't seem logical. The women could make just as much money working close to home. Instead of bedding down in uncomfortable bunks while rolling down long stretches of highway in a pink motor home, they could stay in their own homes with their own families and sleep in their own beds. Yet rather than draw a line in the sand and make the two other band mem-bers come around to her way of thinking, Laura boarded the RV the next time it pulled out.

Though she began the year, as always, touring with the Chicks, Laura's enthusiasm was not what it had been. Neither was her relationship with Martie and Emily. When she fell through an old stage in Muleshoe, Texas—it literally broke open under the very petite woman's weight—she must have wondered if the Lord wasn't giving her a sign. When she realized the Chicks had been booked to perform at a show in Butte, Montana, where the big event that week was the "post-branding testicle festival and horseshoe contest," she had to figure that the band was never going to play anything more than second-rate clubs and casinos with bingo games.

Yet, discouraged and humbled as she was, Laura also loved performing. It was a bug that had caused her to divorce the real world and dive headlong into the gypsy life of the road. Even as she longed for her daughter and Dallas, she had to wonder if she could be satisfied selling real estate or stocks and bonds after dancing with the President of the United States and signing autographs for thousands of people who told her she was the prettiest woman they had ever seen.

In the Texas panhandle the Chicks' motor home lost its transmission. It was just another in a long line of major expenses and delays caused by trying to play the road while earning peanuts. Breaking down one more time was not the straw that broke Laura's commitment to the band, but it didn't make it any stronger, either. The joy and happiness the Dixie Chicks had once brought to her now seemed to be slowly draining away. In a way, she was dying. In February, when she still wasn't able to dig herself out of her emotional hole, Lynch and the Erwins had a meeting that resulted in Laura leaving the band.

Looking back in 1999, Emily told *Country Music* magazine, "The truth is Martie and I started to feel limited creatively." She then added, "We felt we needed the next caliber singer. We talked to Laura. We knew she was getting sick of not progressing further than we had. She had a teenage daughter, and road life was really wearing her down. She said she didn't want to keep going unless something happened. She understood we had to make a change."

Rumors circulating around Dallas at the time had Lynch being forced out. While it was true she was homesick, she probably wanted to stay with the Chicks and just reduce the time spent on the road. It seems highly doubtful that even a homesick Laura would have admitted to the Erwins or herself that she was not a good enough vocalist to front the band.

Another story concerning Lynch's departure placed the move squarely on her shoulders. Some of those close to the Chicks at the time indicated that Lynch was the one who pulled the plug. If that was the case, then she couldn't have made her move at a worse time. The third album, *Shouldn't A Told You That*, had begun to really catch the interest of three or four of the big record labels. Buddy Lee, the Chicks' booker, had been receiving more inquiries, too. Bigger venues were asking about them, and other bookers were interested in them opening for name acts. Though Laura probably couldn't have known it, the hard work was beginning to pay off.

As Lynch packed her bags and the Erwins began to look for a singer who could take them to the next level, many wondered if maybe a Nashville label had been calling the shots all along—a company that wanted Martie and

Emily but not Laura. Had the Erwins been told they could get a deal if they came to the table alone? Here was yet another unsubstantiated rumor being whispered from Music City to DFW. There was probably some truth in each of the theories of why Laura left the band.

With Laura Lynch leading with her vocals and bass licks, the Chicks had been a strong group. Yet their chemistry might have just not been right for mainstream country music. Chemistry was vital for success. In the past many bands had lost members and had suddenly come together with a new sound. Sometimes even losing a great musician and filling the spot with someone with less talent but new ideas made a band click.

In the early sixties Pete Best was the drummer for a four-piece Liverpool, England, group trying to land a major recording gig. The band had been close, but just couldn't seem to make it over the hump. Pushed out by the three other group members, Best was replaced with a drummer who probably wasn't as talented and certainly wasn't as good-looking as Best. But with Ringo Starr the Beatles took the world by storm. The band didn't get the right mix and feel until Ringo joined the group.

In country music Sawyer Brown had won *Star Search* and landed a record deal in 1984. Though close on several occasions to becoming a major player in the music scene, Sawyer Brown still wasn't considered a front-line band in 1992. At best they were only a good opening act for a name star. Sensing the group was never going to really make a move to the major leagues, Bobby Randall, one of Sawyer Brown's most recognized members, left to take a job with TNN. Without Randall, the band was not really any better, but their continued hard work finally paid off. They soared to the top of the charts with great cuts like "Thank God for You" and "This Time." By the mid-1990s, Sawyer Brown became one of the most awarded bands in Music City. Meanwhile, Randall's series was quickly cancelled by TNN and he drifted out of the spotlight altogether.

Would Laura Lynch become to the Dixie Chicks what Pete Best had been to the Beatles and Bobby Randall had been to Sawyer Brown? Would her departure lead to the Erwins being able to find the right mix to push the last of Nashville's doubts aside?

Though Martie and Emily were special musicians, they simply couldn't carry the band by themselves; neither had a strong enough lead voice to drive a show or a sound. After their "divorce" from Laura Lynch, they immediately began to search for a replacement. The new Chick had to be found quickly and had to possess a special quality and voice so that the change of singer would at least not be a backward step. The pressure was like what they had faced when they cut their third album: there was no room for a mistake. If they signed the wrong person, they probably wouldn't ever have the chance to find another. Their momentum would be lost.

One of the first people they called for advice was steel guitar player Lloyd Maines. Maines's steel had been used on two of the Chicks albums and by almost every producer and group in country music. When rock bands needed a steel guitar player for an arrangement, Lloyd usually got the call. Since 1978, he had also evolved into one of Texas's most important record producers. If anyone knew everything about what was going on and who could sing in country music, it was Lloyd. From his home in West Texas, he kept tabs on everyone.

Maines had a long track record in country music. In the 1950s and 1960s he had played in the Maines Brothers Band. Re-formed in the 1970s, the band was popular in Texas clubs as well as on the Las Vegas strip. Mercury Records pushed them for a while, producing two albums and a couple of charting singles, but the band never quite made it. They really came along just a few years too soon to cash in on the opening for country bands created by Alabama.

When he left the family band, Lloyd became a mainstay with Joe Ely and also a major force in the studio as a sessions player. He told an Austin newspaper why he thought so many people sought him out. "I just try to make the artist feel comfortable, and get the absolute best performance out of everybody I work with. To do that, there's a little psychology involved—you have to make them feel good about what they're doing. But as far as any magical techniques, I don't think I've got any. I go into every project without any kind of preconceived notion of how I want to do it. I try to mold my production around the artist."

So the Erwins visited with their old friend and explained their commitment to making the band work: no matter how long it took, they were going to stick it out. They were now looking for someone who was as energetic and determined as they were—someone who could leave her personal problems at home and hit the road with no regrets or concerns.

The person Maines suggested that they contact was his

daughter, Natalie. Lloyd didn't offer her as a father, but as a professional who had a feel for the kind of person the Dixie Chicks needed at the time.

Natalie Maines was a free spirit whose interests included all kinds of sounds and musical styles, but not cowgirl music. She had listened to the Chicks' recordings because her father had played on them. She had also seen the girls a few times, without being drawn to their music. She later told writer Michael McCall, "I was always impressed at how well Martie and Emily played, but as far as the cowgirl music they were playing, I wasn't really into that."

At the time, Natalie wasn't much into school, either. She'd changed her major four times and tried three different colleges. She had even spent time at the world-renowned Berklee College of Music in Boston, before migrating back to the Texas panhandle and Texas Tech University in Lubbock.

Lloyd Maines had a demo tape he had made for his daughter when she had auditioned for a Berklee scholarship. The tape had done its job the first time, getting the family a big financial break for Nat's schooling. But because the demo was light years away from country music, even Maines had to question whether Martie and Emily would be able to hear much mainstream country potential in Natalie's voice. Yet the women liked the demo enough to call Natalie at school and ask her to put together another tape for them.

"Martie and Emily had always been the best part of the Dixie Chicks," Natalie later explained in a news release accompanying the revamped band's first album. "I had been waiting for my shot. I loved watching them play. I didn't know what I was going to do. I just knew I wanted to sing."

"We knew we weren't going to leave each other high and dry," Emily recalled. "Martie and I really started thinking about what we wanted. We were really at the point where we were wanting that major-label success."

"We also knew we needed a lead singer," Martie added.

"So they called and asked if I'd sing on a demo tape," Natalie explained. "So I sang the song 'You Were Mine' and started getting the feeling like I was at an audition."

When the women got together and talked seriously for the first time, Maines still didn't know the real reason she was cutting demos and was being asked so many questions. She had yet to put it all together. In the course of the conversation the Erwins finally demanded to know if Maines really liked country music. When she replied that she loved it, the sisters came back with another question: "Do you think you would ever want to sing it?" Natalie indicated that even though she had classical training, if she was given the chance she would drop everything to make money singing country music. Her reply might have surprised the Erwins, who at first didn't seem to know what to make of Natalie Maines, but it would hardly have been a surprise to those who knew her well. In second grade Nat had told a teacher she didn't need to know anything about math, because she wasn't going to need to use it: she was going to be a famous singer. She may have survived elementary and high school with this attitude but it did help close the curtain on college.

A few weeks after the Erwins heard her first demo,

Natalie officially received the invitation and became a Dixie Chick. Quitting Texas Tech, she packed her bags and, with her father's blessing, moved to Dallas. Less than a week later, she had been through several hard-hitting rehearsals and was on stage in Florida with the Chicks.

Born in Lubbock on October 14, 1974, Natalie replaced Emily as the baby chick. A platinum blonde who looked almost punk, she was barely five foot three and presented a stark contrast to the willow, naturally blond Erwins. Her musical influences included no bluegrass, but a lot of James Taylor, Bonnie Raitt, the Indigo Girls, and Maria McKee. On stage since the age of three, often singing with her father's bands, she was a vocalist, period, with no real instrumental skills. A reformed flower child, a high-school cheerleader, and a loud extrovert, she seemed to have very little in common with the bluegrass-based musicians who wanted her in their band. Yet as bizarre as the chemistry might be, it worked.

When Natalie signed on as a member, the last vestiges of the cowgirl look faded away. The women would soon be wearing on-the-edge clothing that might have been chosen by an L.A. rock band or a Detroit soul group. Their makeup became much brighter too. For the first time, their look was as *electric* as their sound.

"When Natalie joined, she said, 'I dig your music, but I'm not wearing stupid clothes,'" Emily later explained. "At the time, the cowgirl thing was really a gimmick. I mean, as far as being who you are, I'm not a cowgirl. So we kind of re-created ourselves."

Yet the newcomer didn't stop with the clothing; she

pushed for a bolder sound too. She wanted to rock, even if it meant dumping the bluegrass sound altogether. Just because she was the new kid on the block and the youngest chick in the nest, she wasn't going to compromise. If Maines was going to put her stamp on the group, then the other Chicks were going to have to come along too.

Seemingly overnight the women became modern vamps who played hot music. Once Maines joined the group, no one would ever call them cowgirls again. Dale Evans would have never worn fringed bra tops and slit-to-the-thigh skirts. Yet these new Chicks did just that.

The new Chicks were like nothing that had ever hit the road in country music, and they seemed more determined than ever to steamroll to the top. With Maines in charge of the vocals and pushing for a hotter sound, the labels were going to have to take note or get run over. No longer were these women going to take no for an answer. In the past their look and their music had often made people laugh; now both stopped people in their tracks. The sound was driven by an energy that might have always been there, but hadn't been allowed to shine until Nat took charge. As the new Dixie Chicks began to fly, the fans and the press started to say these women had moxie. They impressed fans old and new and even might have intimidated a few: with their new bright flash, many old friends were almost scared to approach them.

Someone who might have been blown away by the changes but wasn't intimated at all was pharmaceutical salesman Ted Seidel. No matter how much time Martie had to spend on the road and how hot the band got, he wasn't going to take no for an answer and wasn't going to put off making her his wife. During the course of a busy travel schedule, he did just that, and Martie became the first of the Erwin girls to start a nest of her own. Yet from the first, her new home didn't seem to be Martie's main focus. Even as a newlywed, her life still centered around her music.

Natalie was also dating someone, but she was going with a man inside the profession. Austin musician Michael Tarabay was a part of her life, but she was not about to let her feelings for him get in the way of career opportunities. As long as he stayed in the background and didn't make too many demands on her time, Natalie would let him hang around.

Emily was getting more than her fair share of male attention too, but at this point the only marriage she was looking for was the one between band and record label. And for the first time in a couple of years, there looked to be a chance that things might come together, too.

Maines was the attention grabber the Chicks needed. She might not have had Laura Lynch's soft beauty, but she was hot and different. She was also young and in tune with the kids who were listening to country music. Finally, she was not caught up in trying to be true to her own musical heritage. Bluegrass meant nothing to her, and she didn't consider her music "art." In Nat's view music was fun set to a melody and a beat. As she seemed to have few expectations beyond that and no baggage to get in the way of her goals, this new Chick was setting her own course and dragging the other band members along.

A number of the Dixie Chicks' old fans, especially the

ones who had followed the group because of its retro look and sound, thought they looked cheap. With her bleached hair and punkish outfits, many of their old Dallas followers figured the Erwins had fallen under a bad influence. They predicted that Natalie Maines would end the Chicks' reign in Dallas as well as their quest for national recognition. Yet the shock value of Natalie's style, as well as her vocal strength, was having just the opposite effect. Not only were the Chicks still overwhelmingly Dallas's favorite band, but Music City was taking another look, too.

From the first day they rehearsed with Natalie, the Erwins had sensed a different climate and attitude. It was like they had suddenly shifted gears. The suggestions the new Chick was making about everything from clothes and hairstyles to music to staging excited them. There was a passion now that went beyond just playing music. Natalie had a burning desire for getting the most out of every moment. She just seemed to love life and not be concerned about problems at all.

With Maines on board, the road trips were more like high-school slumber parties than work details. Natalie always had something to talk about, and she could usually spot something to make them giggle. The fact that the band was having fun while growing made the need to be noticed in Nashville seem less immediate. For the first time in a long time, the unpredictability of not only the road but a music career in general was invigorating rather than draining. If it took a few more years to get their big break, that suddenly didn't seem so bad.

"The big change is Natalie," Emily and Martie told

fans and media who asked why the women now seemed to have so much fire in their bellies and their music. "When she came on, things just picked up."

Anyone who watched the Chicks' lead singer jump around on stage and lead the crowd in joyous exclamations of applause and laughter could have easily guessed she had once been a high-school cheerleader. Yet what the crowds would never have guessed was that she hadn't spent that much time in the spotlight at live shows: she'd been singing since her youth but had never been in charge. Yet leading the band and working the audience came naturally to her. The fact that she rarely picked up her guitar, leaving her free to roam the stage and use her energy and arms to pump up the audience, seemed to enhance her talents as a showwoman and a vocalist.

Yet maybe above all, what Maines brought to the Dixie Chicks was a style and sound that just couldn't be compared to anyone else's. Fans had always said that Robin and Laura sounded like Emmylou Harris, Mary Chapin Carpenter, or other well-known artists. Their look always seemed to remind fans of other people too. Yet with Natalie, there were no contemporary female country music comparisons at all. She was simply unlike anyone else who had ever set foot on a country music stage. Maybe Mark Miller, the acrobatic ball-of-fire leader of Sawyer Brown, had the most in common with Nat, but probably even he couldn't have kept up with her.

As the year moved on and the Chicks played the dates Buddy Lee had lined up for them, Nashville's and country music's inability to put the women into a slot began to pay dividends. Not only did Maines have people talking, but the sound that she brought with her had them listening too.

The reviews were certainly a great deal different now than they had been even a year before. While the Erwins' picking skills were still mentioned by everyone who caught the Chicks live, "bluegrass" was no longer used as a way to describe their sound. Now, rather than being too rural and old-fashioned for Nashville, since Maines's arrival the Chicks might have crossed the road beyond mainstream and wandered over to the rock side of the equation. From Nat's leaping from one side of the stage to the other, to Emily's balancing a fiddle on her nose, there was an unpredictability to the Chicks that had never been there before. When they played in one spot for four or five days at a time, many fans came back night after night just to see what the show was going to be like the next time. The women were so spontaneous, one performance was rarely like another.

Mirian Longino, writing for the *Atlanta Journal*, caught the Chicks' show and wrote, "The Texas trio is as fresh as a clean sheet of notebook paper and may well rewrite the rules of country to include women as not only sequined front singers, but in-the-band pickers as well."

Another reviewer, DJ Kidd Kraddick, added, "The Dixie Chicks are like the Lennon Sisters on acid."

Shirley Jinkins, longtime entertainment voice of the *Fort Worth Star-Telegram*, had followed the Chicks from their beginnings. Since 1992 she had wondered if and when they would get their break and land a deal in Music City. Yet Jinkins hadn't seemed sure it would happen until Maines arrived. The Dixie Chicks had always been good, but now they finally seemed to have a modern sound and a focused direction, too. They seemed like a unified team with a plan. When Jenkins asked Martie if they ever had any doubts about making it in the music business, the newly married Ms. Seidel answered, "Oh, sure, you have your doubts, but it was all new to us, so we had no preconceived notion. And to us, what we were doing on that scale was fun."

Fun was the operative quality Nat had brought to the group. The new lead singer hadn't changed the fact that touring was still hard work, but because she brought such joy into every performance, the other two band members found themselves suddenly blessed with a great deal more patience. It's much easier to wait for the future when your present is so happy!

Martie explained to Jenkins how the change from cowgirls to country rockers had come so rapidly. "When Natalie joined, of course the sound became dramatically different."

The Erwin sisters had no problem with either sharing the spotlight with the newest Chick or giving her a lion's share of the credit as well. Martie and Emily knew the change they had witnessed in both crowd reaction and critical response had been because of Natalie Maines. The painful split with Laura now seemed fully justified.

When the Dixie Chicks had first begun playing in 1989, the word on the Dallas street was that "you have to see them live! You won't believe them!" In 1995, fans were saying the same thing, but this time the reason wasn't Dale Evans outfits and long-forgotten yodeling techniques: it was sexy costumes, a one-of-a-kind rocking-country-boogie sound, hot licks from the band, and enough onstage energy to fuel a jet plane. The old Chicks had won over a small base of Dallas fans by being a laid-back novelty act. When Natalie Maines came on board, the new Chicks began winning over the nation by being a hot act with a novel sound.

The first ten months with Maines at the lead didn't land the Chicks a record deal, but they came much closer to that goal. Now, combining the influences of Bob Wills, Bonnie Raitt, Linda Ronstadt, and a dozen other musical legends from all over the board, the Dixie Chicks were a whole new group. With momentum and a message, they finally appeared fully ready to knock Music City's movers and shakers on their tails.

The U-turn that got Emily a ticket had initiated a year in which the Chicks themselves would take a radical U-turn as well. Laura was gone, Natalie was in. The old sound was history and a new one was on the front burner. The Dixie Chicks were cooking and were about ready to serve a new dish to Nashville and mainstream country radio.

8

The Songbirds Land
a Record Deal

fter plucking strings for seven years and changing musical directions at least three times, the Dixie Chicks exploded into 1996 with a new aggressiveness. A typical concert review read: "The DCs are a breath of fresh air in a world of mascaraoverdosed sex-bombs and wounded ingenues." Translation: It's about time that country music welcomed a new kind of female act to the stage, and the Chicks are that act!

Two decades before, in the early 1970s, Barbara Mandrell had brought a previously unknown energy and life to the ranks of women in country music. Barbara was different, unique, and she expanded the thinking that women were more than just dainty little packages who opened for the men stars. In Mandrell, Music City had a complete performing package wrapped in a female form that took a backseat to no man.

Since Barbara first lit up country music, the world had changed a great deal. Women had arrived in Nashville in huge numbers during the 1980s and 1990s. Yet as more and more of them found record deals, their style and music began to take on the same kind of feel that had once labeled them just "girl singers." Few of them played instruments on stage; almost all of them seemed intent of trying to outdramatize each other on soaring love ballads or cutesy gimmick songs. The fact was Reba McEntire clones were everywhere. Fans would turn on the radio and then wait for a disc jockey to inform them which Reba clone was singing. After a decade of female growth, Nashville had begun to move backward toward the safe women performers of the past, singers who stood behind a microphone and charmed the fans with their beauty and vocal talent, not with their energy and enthusiasm. By the late 1980s, the art of really entertaining an audience had been largely deeded over to men in big hats and all-male bands. Most of Music City's women seemed to lack real energy and dynamic stage passion. They didn't sell anything but their voices and their beauty.

On the other side of the musical coin, the women of rock had become very energetic. A lot of what they were doing on stage and in videos, as well as singing about, couldn't be played on prime-time television; it was a clear signal that women rockers were trying to beat the men at their own game. These entertainers weren't just clones of the women who had come before them; they were women trying to break down barriers and make a play for real power to control their lives, careers, and modes of self-expression.

In the 1970s and early 1980s Mandrell had offered Nashville a challenge that the industry couldn't really duplicate with anyone other than Barbara's younger sister Louise. Barbara had played a long list of instruments, was very attractive, possessed natural charm, and had a great sense of how to style a song and entertain an audience. There were few men or women who could have done what Barbara did onstage more or less two hundred nights a year for a decade.

Yet Reba, the woman who replaced Barbara in the mid-1980s as country music's queen, was a different story. There was no denying that McEntire was a great singer, whose sound and vocal style set her apart from the other up-and-comers of the day. The Oklahoma redhead was an original. Not only did women love her; they gravitated to her and saw this college graduate as a spokesperson for their dreams. Yet because each year Reba had to use larger and fancier sets and stage shows just to top herself on the concert trail, rather than wowing her audiences with guitar riffs and dance steps, it was much easier for Music City to find women who could "be like Reba" than ones who could be like the former queen, Ms. Mandrell. As the long list of McEntire sound-alikes landed record deals, the freshness that Barbara and then Reba had brought to country music faded. This desire to find the next Reba shut the door on almost anyone who was an original. It would be a decade before the next female rolled into Tennessee and dramatically altered producers' thinking. That voice belonged to a teenager from Texas, LeAnn Rimes.

Rimes, with her youth and huge vocal talent, brought to Nashville a goldmine of potential. Yet, rather than be satisfied with the fact that the teen was unique, Music City began a search for a host of teens who could sing like LeAnn. The pattern of inbreeding of styles started again. It appeared as though country music was about to be locked into another boring cycle that not only shut out solid new acts with great potential, like the Dixie Chicks, but diminished the talents and impact of the artists who were currently signed to the recording companies.

Just when the Chicks needed for one of the labels to show the courage it took to sign an act that was radically different from the crop of female LeAnn and Reba wannabes, Shania Twain landed a gig with Mercury Records. Her number-one single "Any Man of Mine" would begin a string of hits that blew the doors off Music City's conservative thinking. Twain was everything a country music performer was not supposed to be, but she still sold product like no one except Garth Brooks ever had. With her controlling the charts like no other male or female in the 1990s, the rules finally had to change.

In a genre dominated by southern-born acts, Shania Twain was a Canadian. In a musical world that wouldn't even acknowledge a teenager like LeAnn Rimes until she had proven her worth and power through years of working on the road, Twain not only hadn't toured, she announced she wasn't going to for a couple more years. In a musical community where only a few well-known producers had controlled the business and artists for years, Shania had roared into town using Mutt Lange, a producer whose resumé didn't include George Jones, Tammy Wynette, or

Garth Brooks but Def Leppard, the Cars, and Foreigner. And Mutt was not only Shania's producer, he was her husband and manager. Having your husband in charge of your career had often gotten you unofficially blacklisted in Music City.

Finally, the Twain image, seen mainly via videos and publicity pictures, had more in common with *Playboy* than with *Country America* magazine. She unabashedly sold sex. One of her first videos was even produced by the king and queen of soft-core titillation, John and Bo Derek. Yet even though she broke all the rules, Shania knocked Reba from her throne and ruled country music and became country music's perfect female power broker.

Twain's incredibly quick climb to the top of the country music charts fueled some new thinking in Nashville. Suddenly acts that had not been given a fair shake because they were not mainstream country seemed to have some potential. Being daring and different actually got you noticed rather than ignored. As the Dixie Chicks were the most radically different band in all of country music, those in search of the next Shania Twain act had to look these women up.

Back home in Texas, as Shania was rewriting the rule book, the Dixie Chicks had remained the region's hottest band. Now, even with their new look and sound, Lone Star fans were lining up to catch them whenever and wherever they could. Teens and college kids were now showing up in droves too. As it watched the new version of the Chicks spread their wings and take flight, the *Fort Worth Star-Telegram* declared the women now really were "ever so close to becoming big stars." The newspaper pointed out that with Twain and Rimes shaking Music City's thinking and structure from the labels to the radio programmers, the time seemed perfect for a group like the Dixie Chicks to find a recording home to call their own. The paper pointed out that the Chicks had been "on the periphery of national notoriety for a half a decade now." Because so much had changed so quickly, the *Star-Telegram* and nearly everyone else in DFW actually dared speak of a pending deal. No longer was the question if the Chicks would get a deal but when.

As the Chicks continued to work the road, as they tried out new material and pushed their stage costuming to include even wilder looks, their name began to finally fit them. They looked like Valley chicks who twanged when they spoke. The look and their mix of blues, country, rock, and bluegrass shouldn't have worked anywhere but counterculture clubs in Greenwich Village or San Francisco, but regular country music fans were buying into it (that is, if there was such a thing as "regular" country music anymore).

One of the things that thrilled the band was that not only were their audiences growing, but the growth seemed to come from fans their own age or younger. Like Shania, the Chicks were bringing a new audience to country music. At their shows, Natalie, Martie, and Emily were seeing kids who didn't even know who George Jones was. These new fans had never heard of country, but they had really gotten into Chick Power.

As the year wore on, more and more of the teenage girls who came to the shows began dressing like the performers. Natalie got into this fan adoration and began asking each new audience, "How many chicks are there out there tonight?" Each night the roar grew louder.

T-shirts that said CHICK POWER began to fly off their concession tables. So did buttons that proclaimed CHICKS KICK ASS! The new attitude Maines had brought to the band had spread to the fans as well.

With the rush of teens to their shows, a fan club mailing list now topping six thousand, and the sales of their three independent CDs now passing sixty thousand units, the women felt as though they were on the brink of hitting the big time. But, even if Nashville didn't call them, they were having so much fun it almost didn't matter. If there was such a thing as a country music cult favorite, the Dixie Chicks would have ruled that roost.

The fact that teens and young adults were turning on to the Chicks probably had a great deal to do with a growing interest by the record labels. Shania Twain had sold more records in her first year on the charts than Patsy Cline had in her entire lifetime. A huge percentage of these sales were young people rather than traditional country music buyers. Alabama had once landed a record deal and fueled millions of dollars in easy profits for RCA by tapping into this overlooked market as well. If teenagers and Generation Xers were beginning to catch Chick Fever, then the potential the trio offered the music industry was well beyond that of any traditional act.

The label that finally took the longest look at the Dixie Chicks and their audience, then brought the women to the negotiating table, was Columbia Nashville. Owned by Sony, Columbia had been thinking about reviving the old country music label called Monument. The company needed an act to anchor this historic comeback. They also needed to sign someone who could generate a lot of press and fan talk. The label set its sights on the Dixie Chicks.

If Sony had come to the Dixie Chicks just a year earlier, the band would probably have cut an easy deal. If the label had hit them six years before, the Chicks might have paid for the right to record. But now things were different. Nashville had waited too late to get the Chicks cheap. If Sony wanted them, they were going to have to prove it by digging deep into company pockets.

As the band was brought to the bargaining table, there were a host of huge acts, such as Garth Brooks and Vince Gill, who were interested in having the Chicks open for them. There were other labels playing footsie with them, too. And their fan base was growing with each new show. Attendance for their small-town appearances had more than quadrupled. If Sony wanted them, then the women wanted some guarantees. They didn't want to come on board a label and record some quickie effort or lose their new sound and identity. They'd listen to advice from their new label, but they wanted to call their own shots. And they wouldn't sign any contract that wasn't a long-term deal. They'd seen others mishandled and thrown away quickly in Music City, and the Chicks weren't going to be a one-shot-and-you're-gone group. They were going to be well supported and well financed or they were going to wait for another label to come around to their terms.

In the past, with Robin Lynn Macy or Laura Lynch calling the shots, there probably would have been some internal conflicts that weakened their position. During the earlier two incarnations of the Dixie Chicks, there had always been arguments about which way to go and what to do. Now there was absolutely no dissension between the Chicks, onstage or off. They were in total agreement on everything—including waiting until they got the deal they wanted.

Though others might talk about the past, the Chicks knew that at this point the past and the band's experimenting with other looks and sounds wasn't important. The Macy- or Lynch-led Dixie Chicks had a look and sound so different from the new Chicks', they wouldn't have been tendered an offer by Sony anyway. But Robin and Laura were gone, and it was Natalie Maines who made the difference. Her explosive personality and drive, coupled with her on-the-edge sense of music, had moved the group to the next level. She had separated them from everyone else and had positioned the Chicks to be noticed when Shania knocked down the door. So, when someone pointed out that they didn't really have a set sound and they had migrated from one look to another, the women pointed out that they had what they needed now—a fresh identity.

It would take five months of hard negotiations before the Dixie Chicks and Columbia Nashville finally put together an unprecedented six-album deal. Not since the early 1960s had contracts like this been commonplace, even for veteran acts. For newcomers, this kind of commitment from a label was unheard of. Yet timing is everything in the business world, and the Chicks' timing had finally been perfect.

Sony was serious about making Monument a Music City mainstay again. In the past the label had helped launch the careers of such legends as Dolly Parton, Roy Orbison, Kris Kristofferson, and Larry Gatlin. In the history of country music the label ranked seventeenth in generating hit records, ahead of such well-known imprints as Atlantic, Imperial, Polydor, Sun, and Starday. Besides the Dixie Chicks, Monument had signed Mr. Guitar, Chet Atkins, away from RCA, and folk/country artist Mary Chapin Carpenter. The label seemed poised for great things.

Yet more than the label's history or the other name acts it was adding to its stable, it was the Dixie Chicks that now had Columbia Nashville excited. They had given up a lot, including the potential of millions of dollars in royalties, to the unproven trio. Yet when the powers at Monument looked at the money the kids in the Chicks' audience brought to each show, as well as the passion these young fans felt for the band, they began to believe that they'd made a steal. The gleeful Sony officials shuddered when they considered what would have happened if Mercury — Shania Twain's label — had gotten the Dixie Chicks: there might not have been room for any other label on the charts or in the stores.

Even before they had gotten them into the studio, Sony declared the Chicks to be "the flagship act of the new label." Sony Nashville president Allen Butler explained simply why the women were so important to Monument's future: "These women are the real deal." To the label's way of thinking, the Chicks were so original that they were going to be huge. And if Monument had the real deal, the original recipe for a female country music band, then no other label could sign anything but a clone or an imitation.

As the band was introduced to press and public, Emily

Erwin honestly exhibited both confidence and a feeling of being overwhelmed by all the sudden attention. "We have about four songs we really feel strongly about right now," she told the audience. "Probably the first time in [the studio] we will cut as many tracks as we have songs, pick a single right away, then go back in and record the rest of the material." To many it sounded like the Chicks didn't really have a clue as to what the deal meant.

At the time many quietly predicted that Monument had made a huge blunder by guaranteeing so much and receiving so little in return. Yet the fact that the label didn't really know what to expect from their expensive new act didn't seem to ruffle their feathers at all. "Musically, nobody else is doing quite what they are doing now," Allen Butler happily explained. Yet many still thought he had lost his mind, because even he couldn't define what it was the Chicks were doing. For that matter, neither could they. Yet when the trio found what they wanted, the women promised Butler, they would let him know.

Even in the months before signing the contract, life on the road had changed. They were still going to dates in the old pink barge, and the money hadn't improved that much, but the audiences had a different look. For over a year, since adding Natalie to the mix, the Chicks had become a rocking country band. People who caught them in 1995 came back to their shows in 1996 with friends in tow. Word of mouth was selling seats in every city where they traveled. And no one was calling them a novelty anymore. Now, with their record deal, the press leaped on board as well, and the excitement at their shows grew even greater.

It seemed that Chick Power was everywhere from California to New York, Texas to beyond the Canadian border.

Continuing to push the envelope with even sexier fashion statements and more dramatic arrangements, the Dixie Chicks had evolved into a show band that had critics struggling to find words to define them. Many looked at the wild clothing and blond hair and simply called them Nashville's Spice Girls. This wasn't something the women wanted or appreciated. The Spice Girls were a studio invention, an advertiser's concept put on a stage and given material and scripts. The Dixie Chicks had invented themselves. They had created their own look and sound. They were talented, hardworking, serious musicians. Yet while the Dale Evans look had once seemingly doomed the band to an image as a novelty act, the wild "chix" style now had many thinking they were partying airheads. "Everybody in this band is just passionate about music," said Natalie Maines. "We want people to like us. And I feel like they will. Because I know we are good."

Many now saw the Chicks, with their almost punk costumes, as a trio of Shania Twains. Emily admitted to *Country Weekly* that it would be easy to perceive the Chicks as women selling themselves as sex objects. But she obviously didn't think they were taking it too far. "We don't play the sexy card that Shania does, but we do enjoy glamour," Erwin told the weekly. "I mean, be serious about your music and know what you want to do but have fun with it, too. It is not worth doing if you take yourself too seriously. And part of it is that we're just girly girls who love putting on makeup and getting pretty clothes."

Their label couldn't have cared less what people were writing about them as long as the presses were running. If the fans wanted the women to be country Spice Girls, fine, as long as their record sales kept up with the Brits'. What Monument wanted was for the talk about the Chicks to continue until their work in the studio could speak for itself.

Now the Chicks were being seen a lot in large venues. They were opening for some of the biggest names in the business. Once the mainstream country fans of Garth Brooks or Alan Jackson got over the shock of the women's clothes, they usually liked the group's unique sound. As the year wore on and they were exposed to more and more audiences, the Dixie Chicks became the hottest act to never release a single in country music history.

Natalie, who was now often called the "slutty" Chick because of her bleached hair and Madonna-type outfits, broke thousands of young boys' hearts by deciding to change her marital status. When she got hitched to her current beau, Michael Tarabay, she left Emily as the only single Chick in the nest. Yet marriage wasn't all that was on the new bride's mind. Natalie had taken guitar lessons and, in spite of the fact she had been playing only about six months, got her own endorsement deal with Gibson. However, she still often tossed the instrument down and worked the crowd instead. And she never failed to sing her heart out. Each new audience was quickly won over to the band's music first by Nat's determined, up-front vocalizing. Within minutes of the opening of each new show, she had established the Chicks as a band who knew how to have fun. Just as she'd gotten Martie and Emily to expand their concepts of how to dress and play, Nat seemed able to lead fans over to her way of thinking as well. In truth, Natalie Maines might have completely overshadowed the other two women if it hadn't been for the Erwins' abilities to make their instruments talk. The sisters' picking was so good, the audiences left awed. On many nights it was hard for Garth or whoever was booked to close the show to get the crowd refocused. Once the audience had seen them live, fans just couldn't quit talking about the Dixie Chicks.

There was little doubt that these three women had everything they needed to become legends on the live stage. They were also, as Emily told the press time and time again, "prepared to pay our dues for as long as it took: we were committed to longevity." Yet could they take the sound and drive they had discovered in the past year and a half of working in clubs and concerts and translate that to musical magic in the studio? Music City had seen a host of great live acts who never were able to capture their stage magic in a quiet studio.

As they prepared to head to Nashville and record for a real label for the first time, the Dixie Chicks had to be on an emotional high. Since Natalie had come on board, they had opened for the likes of Garth Brooks, Alan Jackson, and Emmylou Harris. They had played for more fans in one year than they had in the previous six. They had found a sense of style and a commercial sound that they enjoyed playing. Two of the three women had gotten married. Yet if asked what was the most important thing that had happened to any of them, their reply probably would have been their record contract.

Each night, as the group ended their live show with

Tammy Wynette's "Stand by Your Man," the Dixie Chicks had to be relieved to have a major recording company finally standing by them. Now all they had to do was open the doors for women's bands the way Alabama had for country bands almost two decades before. In other words, once again the trio would be asked to do something that had never been done before. Now the group had to convince a few million country music fans and hundreds of radio disc jockeys who had never heard of the Dixie Chicks that Monument Records really had signed the "real deal."

Nineteen ninety six had been a very eventful year for the trio, but for the industry the year had belonged lock, stock, and barrel to Shania. So while the Dixie Chicks now had a recording contract, '96 was simply the calm before the storm. In 1997, the Chicks would have their lives changed in ways none of them ever dreamed of and would begin to radically impact all of the country music industry, too.

9

Songbirds
in the
Studio

n 1997, the Dixie Chicks would begin to learn how things were expected to be done in Nashville, Tennessee. They would learn that their time was no longer theirs. They would also come to understand that the demands they had known in the past were insignificant compared with the demands placed on them now.

Meanwhile, Music City would begin to learn that the Dixie Chicks didn't do things the expected way, so the rules didn't really matter. While the Chicks would work hard and live up to all their new label wanted, the way people reacted to their work would be a great deal different than anything Nashville had ever witnessed. Chick Fever was beginning to take root in the music capital of the world.

As the Monument Record deal was announced, newspapers and magazines displayed stories that presented the trio as an overnight success. A typical lead ran: "The Dixie Chicks were a Lone Star State sensation from the get-go. Virtually overnight, the group was opening for Garth Brooks, Alan Jackson, Loretta Lynn and Emmylou Harris. Public figures such as Ross Perot and George W. Bush were requesting they play at their events." From this starting point the stories would usually continue to paint the group's history as a downhill slide to fame and fortune. Outside of their home turf in Dallas-Fort Worth, few media outlets seemed interested in presenting the fact that the band had spent seven years trying to prove themselves worthy of being signed by a Nashville label. As the Erwins explained to reporters, life during this early period of the band's evolvement had been anything but easy.

While the Erwins would answer any questions about their past work, this hot version of the Dixie Chicks didn't really dwell much on the past. Because of this, as well as the label's new group bio, it often seemed as though even Martie and Emily viewed the real beginning of the Chicks as the day Natalie Maines took over as lead singer.

Monument had big plans for the women's first CD. As the label watched Shania Twain sell millions of albums via sexy, splashy videos and well-placed TV appearances, the record bosses had to figure that they too could easily cash in with their new act. All they had to do was find the right songs to go with the trio's hot look. For that reason almost everyone at Monument was digging for material.

As the Chicks worked the road and prepared for the studio, they discovered how much was expected of an up-and-coming Nashville act. Suddenly, the demand for interviews, appearances, and concerts far exceeded their time. Things like marriages, dating, time with family, and even trips to the mall were put on hold. Show business was their world.

Hank Williams, Jr. once said that country music didn't leave any room for a family life. His statement was a warning to all of those who dreamed about becoming entertainers. If you gave yourself to your career, if you did the things you had to do to give yourself a chance at becoming a star, then you would have to sacrifice any type of conventional life with your loved ones. There would be little quality time for husbands, wives, or children. When at some point a performer finally had a few days off, he'd come home and discover that he had no idea who was living there.

For newlyweds Martie and Natalie, just now beginning lives with their husbands, this new period of heavy demands might have been excruciating. Yet they were probably too busy to notice. In a suddenly exciting world where they were the focal points of almost everything, the fact that they were missing bonding with their mates wasn't so obvious. For the Chicks, it was work from morning until night. The few spare moments they had, when they weren't visiting with the press or doing shows, were spent listening to demos. When they signed the names to the contract, they'd given in to the fact that this first album for Monument had to be the most important thing in their lives.

Chick Fever was beginning to spread even before the women walked into the studio. The band was being talked about on *Crook and Chase* and other entertainment programs as if they were already proven commodities. Monument had to love the fact that many stories on television, radio, and in the press centered on why other record labels had failed to pick up on the Chicks' potential. Jennifer Mendelsohn, a writer for *USA Today Weekend*, cornered *Nashville Tennessean's* country music critic Tom Roland trying to find an answer to why so many had passed on an act that was now being labeled a sure thing. Roland explained, "All these [country music] executives are trying to be safe." He went on to explain that acts such as the Chicks and Twain did anything but play it safe and that this scared much of the establishment.

After more than half a year of touring, the songbirds finally got the chance to show their stuff to their new label. Working with a huge budget and the support of a cast of what seemed like hundreds, the Dixie Chicks experienced what it was like to be treated like recording stars. Monument's producers for the project, Paul Worley and Blake Chancey, wanted to capture the spirit of the real Chicks, not try to reinvent them. Chancey wanted the women to play on every song. He wanted the energy he had seen in performances to come through in the studio. He seemed to feel that the driving music of the Erwins was the key to opening everything else up, too.

While signaling to the Chicks that they thought Martie and Emily to be the equal of any musician in the city, the producers had also signed up some of the industry's best pickers to fill out the musical arrangements. With Mark Casstevens on acoustic guitar, Joe Chemay on bass, Billy Crain on guitar, Lloyd Maines and Tony Paoletta on steel, Greg Morrow as the drummer, Matt Rollings on keyboards, and Billy Joe Walker Jr. and Paul Worley filling out the string band, the session players were topflight indeed. Yet to make sure things went well, the label pulled out the checkbook and added Bobby Charles Jr., another bass player, as well as George Marinelli on electric lead and Tom Roady with additional percussion. This team of professionals, combined with Emily on dobro, banjo, and guitar and Martie on fiddle and mandolin, was a band that Bob Wills would have considered "just about the right size to play anything."

The producers met with the Chicks several times before the first day of recordings. The men wanted to make sure the women felt good about the music and the pickers. They also wanted Natalie, Martie, and Emily to be prepared for both the time it would take to record and overdub each cut and the many times they would have to come back into the studio for follow-up work. Finally, just before D day, Chancey had some final advice. He begged the women to show up in the studio in old clothes. He wanted them to forget their makeup and not worry about their hair, either. He didn't want any hint of sex appeal in the studio: he was afraid that if the women dressed like they did on stage, the sessions players wouldn't be able to fully concentrate on their jobs. It was one of the first times in his life that Chancey had ever been concerned that beauty might turn the recording project into a beast.

One of the biggest challenges the producers would face had little to do with the Chicks' looks, but rather with trying to catch a sound and style that the women had been using for only two years and had never put on a recording. The men had to make sure this hot Chick sound and style was used on each of the new cuts they had chosen to record. Finally, Worley and Chancey had to walk the fine line between directing the trio and staying away from them and letting them determine what each song needed. Though this might have appeared easy to an outsider, it was a daunting job and an enormous responsibility. Monument had a great deal riding on the project. This album would kick-start the label's future. The producers had to make the final product commercial, but in the process they also had to make sure they didn't lose what made the Chicks so special.

The women felt the pressure too. For the first time, they were having to give away some of the duties and responsibilities that they'd grown used to tackling themselves. Scores of people had warned them that their label would try to control everything about their lives, down to the way they looked and sounded, and that was scary too. Some of their fans in Texas even thought the women had sold out their freedom just to have a shot at fame and fortune. "Texas likes to think it has its own musical identity and doesn't like to give up its artists, especially to Nashville," Emily had explained to the Dallas media as she was getting ready to go into the session. "There was a lot of pressure on us when we decided to go to Nashville," she added. "People were worried we'd fall into the 'Nashville trap' and produce records that were too slick."

All fears aside, the sound that would come from the first album would be distinctive and very much what the Chicks had been using since Natalie joined the band. The fiddles and steel guitar riffs would say country, but the vocals were even closer to rock and blues than Shania Twain's were.

Ultimately the studio would name the Dixie Chicks' first Monument effort *Wide Open Spaces*. The title was appropriate. The band had come from the huge state of Texas and had played a lot of places while getting to the point where they were ready to tackle the big time. Few things could better describe the long trail the Erwins had been down than one filled with wide open spaces and a lot of U-turns.

The song chosen to lead off the album was "I Can Love You Better." After much debate, it would also be the cut the label picked as the band's first single. "I Can Love You Better" was written by Kostas and Pamela Brown Hayes. The harmonies that kicked off the number were straight country, but when Natalie picked up the first verse and the rest of the women slid in on the chorus, the song ceased its country feel and became a number that a rockin' Linda Ronstadt might have recorded two decades earlier. With enough country flavor to appeal to country radio, but still possessing the driven sound that had electrified live audiences for the past two years, "I Can Love You Better" was a song that Shania Twain would have loved, too. Not as musical as many of the other cuts picked for the first project, this number was 180 degrees away from everything on the Chicks' first three independent albums. It was a great way to show how much they had grown and evolved.

"I Can Love You Better" was probably chosen as the first single because of songwriter Kostas's recent track record. A native of Greece who'd grown up in Montana, his song "Timber I'm Falling in Love" had been just the ticket Patti Loveless needed to reestablish herself as a country music force. He'd penned Dwight Yoakum's Grammy-winning "Ain't That Lonely," three hits for Martina McBride ("Love on the Loose," "Heart on the Run," and "Life"), and a dozen other major hits for artists like Travis Tritt and McBride and the Ride. In 1990, he was named country music's Songwriter of the Year. Kostas wrote what artists loved, and "I Can Love You Better" seemed to be the kind of song that turned disc jockeys on too.

The album's title cut was a ballad that featured not only Natalie's hard, bluesy vocals but the women's country gospel harmonies. "Wide Open Spaces" was in some ways a song that reflected the Dixie Chicks' history. The band really did need room to grow, as well as a chance to be themselves in a world that yearned for conformists. Written by Susan Gibson, this was one of the cuts that seemed tailor-made for the Chicks. No one who listened to it could ever have pointed to another artist who'd have put a better twist on "Wide Open Spaces." Still, with its rather unmelodic leads and rocking style, few expected that the company would ever release it as a single — much less that it would land in mainstream country's top ten in 1998.

In 1973, Dobie Gray had used "Loving Arms" for chart success on the rock playlists. In 1981, four years after his death, RCA had released Elvis Presley's cut of the song, and the King had hit the top ten on the country charts with it. Natalie Maines had brought the old song to the table and tackled it à la Dobie Gray, rather direct and straightforward. Strangely, this old blues song seemed much more traditional country than almost anything else on the album. It was never released as a single despite its very strong chart possibilities.

It's doubtful that when Tia Sillers and Mark Selby wrote "There's Your Trouble," they thought a female band would earn their first number-one with it. With Martie's pleading fiddle riffs and the women's solid harmonies, this cut was infectious: listeners found it hard not to tap their feet and shake their heads to the drumbeat. Everyone at the sessions must have realized that this cut had chart potential. There was little doubt that country music was going to love "There's Your Trouble." It was incredibly strong, from Martie's fiddle opening to the musical fadeout—the kind of song that got inside people's brains and stayed there all day long.

Sillers and Selby had been good friends for a long time when they began working on "There's Your Trouble." But until one of the two stumbled on the phrase "It should have been easy," this particular writing session had been several hours of wasted effort. Once they came up with the hook phrase, the song came together almost as quickly as the pair could jot down the words. One of the few Music City writing teams who pitched their material to R&B and rock performers, the duo had scored number-one hits on a variety of charts. This song would give their bank balances a huge boost—and send the Chicks to a local tattoo parlor as well.

The fifth cut on *Wide Open Spaces* was a product of the Erwin sisters' own creativity: "You Were Mine." It was a haunting ballad that showed both their incredible writing potential, and the full range of Natalie's vocal talents: a sad, sincere message wrapped in a timeless country melody. Those in the studio just knew that if the Chicks didn't release this as a single, somebody else would pick it up. The song was a natural for radio airplay and screamed for video treatment.

"You Were Mine" had been introduced at a Christmas concert at Billy Bob's nightclub/honky-tonk in Fort Worth, Texas. The Erwin sisters informed the crowd that it was based on a true story but never explained what that story was: their own parents' long marriage and fairly recent breakup. That night, and in many shows thereafter, this ballad was the crowd's favorite number.

Radney Foster and George Ducas collaborated for "Never Say Die." The song began with a deep guitar lead that seemed to be inspired by Duane Eddy, yet any other signs of old rock-and-roll ended there. A cut filled with heartbreak, "Never Say Die" had a Roseanne Cash feel to it. It was a nicely arranged song, but paled in comparison to the number that followed. "Tonight the Heartache's on Me" was a Texas-two-step honky-tonk retro classic that Patsy Cline or Kitty Wells might have cut if they had been given the chance. Natalie's vocals came in cold to kick-start the Mary W. Francis, Johnny Macrae, and Bob Morrison composition. Filled with wailing steel guitar riffs and crying fiddles, "Tonight" was a straightforward country song that would have called any Mel Tillis fan to the dance floor the second he first heard it.

Natalie's bluesy voice again began the Billy Crain and Sandy Ramos rocker "Let 'Er Rip." This song had been a standard at Chicks concerts for some time. With its nod to Bonnie Raitt, no song on the project did a better job of combining the band's diverse styles. In the span of two minutes and forty-nine seconds, the Dixie Chicks combined blues, rock, country, bluegrass, honky-tonk, and gospel and made it all fit together.

"Once You've Loved Somebody" was a Bruce Miller and Thom McHogh–penned cut that seemed to be intended for either Reba McEntire or one of the many clones who tried to wrap their voices around the tragic, soaring ballads that made up so many of the singles released over the past decade by Music City female singers. The harmonies that Natalie, Martie, and Emily hit on the chorus sounded very much like those used by Reba and Linda Davis in both the studio and in McEntire's live performances.

Like the previous cut, "I'll Take Care of You," written by veteran tunesmith John David Souther, is another typical female ballad of the type being used by a host of Music City female acts of the day. The Chicks' rendition was solid and honest, pulling at the heartstrings and selling the message with a sincere straightforward style.

"Am I the Only One (Who's Ever Felt This Way)" was another ballad, this one written by Maria McKee, but it didn't have a modern Nashville feel; it was more pop/folk than country. The instrumentation was the only thing that hinted the song was intended for a Music City audience. Maines, who often employed more than a hint of Linda Ronstadt in her vocals, embraced one of her idol's most common 1970s soulful styles in this song.

The album concluded its dozen cuts with a Bonnie Raitt–penned classic, "Give It Up or Let Me Go." Though the harmonies had an almost gospel feel, vocally this song was really all Natalie Maines. The edge that she brought to the Dixie Chicks was most obvious on this final cut. With solid blues guitar and dobro lead work, the gutsy rockabilly vocals that were often used by Wanda Jackson in the 1950s were employed here by Maines in a style that showed that while she might not have the vocal range of former Chick lead singer Laura Lynch, she had style and punch to die for. With its bare-bones arrangement, "Give It Up or Let Me Go" represented well the fact that the Dixie Chicks were a band, not just another female group.

In her liner note for the album, Emily noted that their producers were an incredible team, and added—a sentiment that seemed at odds with many of the Erwins' past experiences in the recording studio—"Thank you for your hard work, long hours, and making this album the most fun, creative and inspiring experience I've ever had." She went on to acknowledge the people who had driven her all over Texas to shows and music lessons as a child: "To the one unconditional constant in my life—my parents—thank you for the years of lessons, coming to the shows, driving all those miles so we could pay to play, and teaching me that, instead of being the cheerleader, I should be the one in the game."

Natalie began her liner note with a testament to her Christian faith, then acknowledged her mate and her family: "I would also like to thank Michael, for being my perfect match, I love you, my Dad (Homer), and my Mom for all their wisdom, love and support." She concluded by listing her inspirations: James Taylor, Bonnie Raitt, Indigo Girls, Maria McKee, and John Travolta—not a country musician in the lot.

Like her sister, Martie used her note to thank her parents, then acknowledge the two women who worked with her in the band. Her pride could be seen when she simply wrote how the music "moved" her.

It must have seemed ironic to many that Robin Lynn Macy, who had left Domestic Science Club and formed a new group, Round Robin, and Laura Lynch, now remarried and modeling western wear, had been so quickly and completely dismissed and forgotten. At one time they had both been the voices of the Dixie Chicks. Now, like Pete Best, they were lost pieces of history.

Out of the studio, the Chicks were given a three-pronged agenda. First, they had to tour, both fronting for many of Nashville's hottest draws and entertaining on their own at smaller venues. Second, they had to go before the cameras and shoot a fun and fast-paced video to go with the release of "I Can Love You Better." Finally, they had to spend the rest of their waking hours doing radio, print, and television interviews to pump their new album.

Though it might have seemed the most draining element of the plan, the concerts were probably the easiest facet of the Chicks' new agenda. This was just a continuation of what the Erwins had been doing all their lives and Natalie had been doing for the past couple of years. Though the crowds were bigger, performing wasn't new to any of them.

Video work was more of a challenge. The artists had little control over anything, periods of intense work were followed by long periods of waiting, and what should have taken a few minutes always seemed to take hours. This first video was shot at four different locations, all in Nashville:

the airport, a tattoo parlor, a cake bakery, and a downtown street reset to suggest the 1950s. The final result may have looked like a party, but in truth, like most videos, it was an exercise in torture and patience.

Yet, even more than the video, it was the demands of promotion that were hardest on the women. While the Chicks had once prayed that a writer would approach them once or twice a week, now they were doing as many as a dozen interviews a day. They were asked the same questions over and over again and they always seemed to have photographers wanting that special photo for their magazine's story. And as they would soon find out, things were destined to become even more hectic.

Monument rented Nashville's old Ryman Auditorium to host the concert that previewed the Chicks' new album. On this fall evening, the trio of hopeful stars would find themselves performing on country music's most hallowed stage. It was an awe-inspiring place to spotlight their first major album in front of an audience of critics, bookers, industry insiders, and country music fans who really didn't know much about them. All around them, the women could sense and feel the ghosts of country music's greatest stars—legends such as Minnie Pearl, Hank Williams, Ernest Tubb, Marty Robbins, Patsy Cline, and Jim Reeves. It was exciting, eerie, and scary all at the same time. Few newly signed artists had ever been placed in such a bright spotlight right out of the box.

At the Ryman, the Chicks came through like seasoned professionals and kicked their album off with a bang. As word hit the street that not only was *Wide Open Spaces* filled with solid material, it was also much different than what

Music City labels normally produced for country audiences, an excitement began to build both at Monument's offices and on the Chicks' tour bus. For seven years people had been telling the Erwin sisters they were about to hit the big time; now they were so close they could almost touch it. As one PR release bragged, "The Dixie Chicks are a marketable package: three fresh-faced, pretty blondes with a decidedly Southern image, crystalline harmonies, bluegrass pedigree and '90s savvy. How can it go wrong?" Still, as all three Chicks knew, until radio stations and the public embraced the women's sound, there were no sure things, no matter how good the advance word.

When not in the studio, the Chicks were on the go and on the road. The women worked from New York to California and 150 places in between. The band played radio showcases, conventions, holiday bashes, and honky-tonks and opened for the likes of Sammy Kershaw and George Jones. They also worked in two months of radio tours, appearing at every reporting station that would let them in the door. About the only places they didn't get to work were their own homes.

Not long after putting the final touches on their album, the Dixie Chicks attended their first Country Music Association awards show. Viewers of the highly rated CBS special couldn't have known that Monument's hot new band was there. Without official invites from the hosting group, the women found seats in the balcony. There, with the common folks who called themselves country music's biggest fans, the fledgling trio watched the performances, kept track of the awards, and wondered if they would find themselves down closer to the stage a year down the road.

On October 15, 1997, the video of "I Can Love You Better" was first played on Country Music Television. CMT is to country music what MTV is to rock. It was how acts like Shania Twain had pumped up their record work. Video had grown more important to the marketplace for a decade. Now, having a hit video was almost essential in order to score with a hit single. Within days of the debut of "I Can Love You Better," viewer demand was so high that the video had been placed in heavy rotation.

Buoyed by the positive response to the video, twelve days later Monument shipped the single to radio stations. Though they never admitted it publicly, the label was concerned about the Chicks' first single. They had wondered if the rocking dance song would find acceptance by country radio. When almost every station in the country added "I Can Love You Better" on its first week, Monument knew they had guessed right and they had a winner for their anchor group. When the single began flying out of stores in November, all signals pointed to a great forecast for album sales in January.

Just having the record in the can should have made Christmas 1997 the best ever for the three young women. Yet the advance word on *Wide Open Spaces* and the rapid success of their first single were so exhilarating that the holidays were all but forgotten. It seemed that everyone wanted to interview the group that was now being almost universally called country music's Spice Girls. They were hotter than even Santa Claus.

Without much time to contemplate how rapidly things were moving, Martie, Natalie, and Emily found themselves sharing a set with Barbara Walters and company on ABC's hot daytime show *The View*. CNN's *Show Biz Today* did a whole segment with the Chicks, as did *Sally Jessy Raphael*. There were scores of other requests for TV appearances, while corporate sponsors also were on the phone wanting to know if the trio could be a part of their 1998 package tours. Even when they were home, the women's phones never stopped ringing. Never had a country music group become such a hot commodity without even having a hit record yet. But as the year ended and the Dixie Chicks album was about to be shipped, many wondered if this publicity balloon wasn't blowing up too quickly. What if the album didn't live up to the hype?

The Chicks themselves didn't have much time to think about failing; Monument kept them too busy working. So while Natalie, Martie, and Emily wanted to be successful, they must have had to wonder if they could survive the demands promised by a best-selling album and hit single.

Meanwhile, the women put together what would be the final edition of their fan newsletter, *Chick Chat*. They wrote about the blur of activity that defined their last year, admitting that they couldn't really remember all the places they had been and all the things they had done. They also confessed to being homesick.

As they would soon discover, the Dixie Chicks had flown their home coop forever. The simple life of working and then going home was a thing of the past. Natalie, Martie, and Emily were about to find unparalleled success, but it wouldn't come without some unexpected and heartbreaking sacrifices.

10

The Chicks
Find Something
to Crow About

A s the Chicks entered 1998, Martie Seidel listed three goals for the year. To the band's fans the goals might have seemed modest, but to industry insiders they must have looked like long shots. After all, the Chicks were a rookie band, and how much success could virtual unknowns expect after just coming out of the recording studio for the first time with a major label?

The initial item on Martie's wish list was to have a number-one record. Considering that the Chicks were women and that women in general had not been performing too well on the charts recently, this was not an easy goal at all. And having a chart topper right out of the box was almost unheard of. Only two women had ever done it: Connie Smith in the 1960s and Faith Hill in 1994. It had taken Reba five years and fourteen singles to earn her first number one. In fact, many award-winning country music performers had enjoyed long and distinguished careers without ever seeing the top of the charts. Mac Davis, Brenda Lee, and Lacy J. Dalton were all major award winners, but none of them ever hit number one. The list of shutouts was long and distinguished. In rock, even the much-loved Creedence Clearwater Revival had never earned a chart-topping single.

Martie Seidel—she was now officially going by her married name—also wanted to earn a gold album. In 1996, this goal might actually have been easier to achieve than landing at the top of the singles charts. Because of the recent boom in country music sales, more and more artists had been able to reach gold. Yet timing indicated this would be tougher in 1998 than just a few years before. Shania and LeAnn had done remarkably well in 1997, but almost all other acts' sales had dropped. The industry as a whole would have slipped into a major depression without Twain and Rimes taking up the slack. So gold would be a big step as well.

Finally, Martie indicated that the Chicks wanted to end the year by receiving a nomination from the Country Music Association. To receive a nomination the band was going to have to impress the voters in a real hurry. Initial ballots went out early in the summer. This gave the women just five months to have enough success on the charts, on the radio, and at live performances to turn the voters' heads. As it turned out, that would be plenty of time for the dynamite band from the Lone Star State.

With great anticipation and perhaps a bit of dread, the

Dixie Chicks looked forward to the release of *Wide Open Spaces*. Certainly the success of the band's first single, "I Can Love You Better," indicated that the women could expect some solid initial sales of the album. But the news was better than just a solid number. In an almost unheard-of move, the album jumped onto the charts during its release week at number 17—one of the highest debuts in country music history, and the most successful opening ever for a new act. Monument and the Chicks must have been completely blown away. When, at almost the same moment, "I Can Love You Better" jumped into the top ten, it seemed time to party.

One of the best places to get a read on what buyers were thinking was at the nation's largest retailer of country music, Wal-Mart. The discount chain was seeing a major run on *Wide Open Spaces*. In stores across the nation reorders were coming in almost too fast for Monument to fill them. Many Wal-Mart Supercenters were dedicating several rows of product displays just for the hot new country band. The best news about the chain's remarkable initial sales was that the consumers who were purchasing the Chicks' music were younger than normal country buyers. The trio was appealing to the Shania and Garth crowd.

As much as the initial sales reports were cause for celebration, sustaining that initial burst would be much harder and depend upon a great deal more than just one single and the band's unique reputation as outstanding live performers. While fans often bought music on impulse, if they didn't like what they purchased, they shared the news with others. With bad word of mouth, sales dropped flat. The second wave of buyers would also be influenced by reviews. So would a lot of radio programmers and wholesale buyers for record chains. If the reviews were overwhelmingly good, then orders for *Wide Open Spaces* would increase dramatically. When the critics liked an entire package, it gave the release "legs."

While it was easy for Reba and Garth to get reviewed, most new acts had to duke it out with a host of other releases for ink. Monument realized that many established critics might pass on the Chicks altogether. Yet if the PR department was able to generate a few votes of confidence from solid and respected sources, it would be a great sign for the album and the Chicks. While the label prayed for a handful of good mentions in the press, they would soon be blown away by more reviews than they'd believed possible.

USA Today was one of the first major publications to review the album. As the nation's most-read newspaper usually only hit one country release a week, Monument had to be pleased just to earn a mention. When the label read the paper's review, they must have been thrilled. In a glowing tribute *USA Today* wrote: "The eclectic tendencies of fiddle/mandolin player Martie Seidel, multi-instrumentalist Emily Erwin, and vocalist Natalie Maines fit nicely into Monument's legacy of country and pop. . . . The Dixie Chicks are shaping up to be the first breakout country act of 1998."

The *Tennessean*, Nashville's most-read newspaper, probably understood and appreciated country music better than any daily in the nation. The paper wrote: "The Dixie Chicks provide a cool, three-part feminine harmony with a spunky attitude that draws casually on plenty of influences, while keeping a sound all its own. . . . The Dixie Chicks have the ability to take country's already strong women into even edgier territory."

People magazine, whose reporters would soon be covering the band through feature articles, stated, "This is an old-fashioned, good-time album, affable and rich with sweet-toned melodies."

Monument could have run to the bank on those first tributes alone, but they wouldn't have to. The good news kept coming, not only from newspapers in the United States but from north of the border as well. "This is one of the most refreshing debuts to come down the line from Music City in some time," wrote the *Windsor Star* critic. "Every song on this plate, and there are twelve of them, is either dipped in a hardcore country vat or a folkie meets country glaze. No new country pounding here."

Half a continent away the *Atlanta Journal* added, "This all-woman group is as fresh as rolling down the windows after being strapped in the pickup with boring pop wannabees (Bryan White, Shania Twain) all year. Keep an eye on this group." In the *Tribune Review* came these gratifying words, "Maines, Seidel and Erwin have been working at their musical careers for years, both together and separately. With the impressive *Wide Open Spaces*, they display a winning combination that should keep their star rising fast."

The *Cleveland Plain Dealer* agreed. The respected Ohio paper called the album "a perfect example of how to make undeniably contemporary country music that remains deeply rooted in the music's history and traditions. This album has more spunk, chutzpah, individuality and raw instrumental skills than a whole bin of today's typical Nashville releases."

Back home in Texas, the *Dallas Morning News* had been the group's most vocal cheerleader since the days when the women dressed up like Dale Evans and sang almost pure bluegrass. As many of the Chicks' fans from those days now felt the women had sold out their honest and pure sound to earn a chance at radio play, it was expected that the *News* would be less than glowing in its assessment of the Chicks' first mass-market venture. In fact, the leading newspaper in the Lone Star State loved it. The review included high praise such as " 'I Can Love You Better,' the first radio hit from Dallas' Dixie Chicks' major-label debut, is the most infectious introductory single since Trisha Yearwood burst onto the national scene in 1991 with the irresistible ode to small-town romance, 'She's in Love with the Boy.' . . . Propelled by Emily Erwin's homespun dobro and banjo work, Martie Seidel's potent fiddle and mandolin solos and lead singer Natalie Maines' in-your-face vocals, *Wide Open Spaces* lives up to its title. . . . The new sound gives the Chicks room to roam those wide open spaces."

By now Natalie, Martie, and Emily might have been tired of all the good news. Yet their label wasn't. Each day Monument's staff anxiously awaited the next batch of clippings. With each new shipment, there were more glowing words. In many cases it seemed like newspapers weren't just reviewing the album but writing feature-length stories about it. The reviews were longer than most of the regular country music articles that ran in many of the publications. Never in their wildest dreams had anyone expected this kind of response to *Wide Open Spaces*.

"This is one band of chicks who don't intend to get carried along by their cover-girl looks. They have talent and substance to boot," wrote *American Country* magazine. The *Austin American Statesmen* added, "The good news is that their sojourn to Nashville has yielded an album that retains much of the Chick's freewheeling exuberance while applying a commercial sheen to an undeniably marketable product."

Music reviewer Sarah Rodman wasn't wild about Sparkle's new release and thought Loretta Lynn's daughters need a lot more work, too. But on the same day she panned two albums, the critic relished what the Chicks had accomplished, as well as how much Monument had put into this initial release. "Rich harmonies, wry interpretations of some of Nashville's best songwriters' wares and tasteful playing from all three Chicks makes this pop-country at its best."

The well-respected Canadian scribe Fish Griwkowsky added, "But can they perform? Well, the band's suggestive name and album title certainly suggest so and the fact is they're g-r-r-reat, as Tony the Tiger would growl, probably before eating them if he was a real tiger . . . We have a winner!" And the *Edmonton Journal* went on for a half a page with high praise for the release. As the comparisons to the Spice Girls had been tossed in the Dixie Chicks' faces for months, Peter North's lead comments must have meant a great deal to the trio. "No, these three lovely ladies are thankfully not Nashville's answer to the Spice Girls. This is instead one of the most refreshing debuts to come down the line from Music City in some time. . . ."

Another Canadian, James Muretich of the *Calgary Herald*, also took a half-page reviewing *Wide Open Spaces*. He concluded his overview: "The result is a refreshing debut disc that catches the unsuspecting listener off guard, delivers the goods and gets you pulling out your old Emmylou Harris, Dolly Parton and Loretta Lynn records." Muretich echoed what more than ninety percent of the critics wrote about *Wide Open Spaces*. These positive reviews set the table for huge orders and reorders from distributors.

Even a few sour apples couldn't stop the momentum now. In the *Philadelphia Inquirer* the Dixie Chicks failed to impress a nameless critic: "Trouble is," the paper printed, "the Chicks have compromised their distinctiveness to pursue the dubious goal of becoming inoffensive radio fodder." Mark Guarino, a suburban Chicago reviewer, didn't like the trio, either. He noted that "the Chicks are about as revolutionary as Shania Twain's leather pants. While most of their debut is embedded with acoustic instruments, the overwrought singing and obvious lyrics make this album business as usual for pop country radio playlists." And in the *Baltimore Sun* J. D. Considine scored the release a bomb, giving it only one and a half stars.

But the few negative voices couldn't come close to dampening the spirits at Monument. The label was forcing Sony's CD and tape plants to work overtime just to keep up with new orders. Within a month the album had reached the top ten and everyone was crowing. "The Dixie Chicks are a perfect example of how great music shines through," exclaimed Sony's senior vice-president of sales and marketing, Mike Kraski. "Natalie, Martie, and Emily are incredible musicians and they have created a totally unique and thrilling album with *Wide Open Spaces* . . . and obviously the consumer agrees."

The smash album meant that the Chicks—who were traveling extensively, already having been booked for more than two hundred shows—were now in even greater demand. Magazines, newspapers, television and radio shows wanted them whenever they had a spare moment. Yet even more than the media, the fans wanted the band and their hot new sound.

The first single, "I Can Love You Better," had stalled at number 7. But as very few acts had ever taken their initial release to the top ten, this was still a remarkable achievement. And the video hit number one on CMT, so in a way the women did have a chart topper right out of the box.

Monument celebrated the good reviews and the sales news by sending out thousands of postcards with the Chicks pictured walking across a road. On the front of the photo was written, "Why did the Chicks cross the road?" The backside read:

a. To have a #1 Video @ CMT, "I Can Love You Better."
b. To have a Pick Hit @ CMT, "There's Your Trouble" (just released with the single soon to follow).
c. To perform the "Tammy tribute" at the ACM's.
d. All of the above.

The answer was, of course—all of the above. The fact that the Chicks had been picked to sing "Stand by Your Man" on the Los Angeles–based Academy of Country Music's nationally televised award show would be not only a big push for their album and soon-to-be-released single, but a great introduction to the CMA voters as well.

Rather than stop and enjoy the fact that the Chicks had so much going their way, Monument pushed another single and video. "There's Your Trouble" was released in March. This song didn't just keep *Wide Open Spaces* hot, it made the album even hotter. When fans heard this record, they hit music outlets in record numbers. Within two months "There's Your Trouble" was in the top ten.

The success of the singles and the album made it hard for the Country Music Association voters to ignore the Dixie Chicks. When the initial ballots came in, the Chicks had made the first cut in several categories.

In early June, at country music's annual celebration for its fans—a week-long festival called Fan Fair—more than forty-thousand rabid music lovers showed up to meet the stars, watch concerts, take pictures, and get autographs. The Chicks had been popular with a small segment of the crowd in 1997, but many more fans had sought out Bryan White and Faith Hill than Natalie, Martie, and Emily. In 1998, the DCs were the draw. Thousands stood in line for hours just to get their signatures and meet them face to face. But then, long lines were now the norm everywhere the Dixie Chicks appeared.

The speed at which things were happening caught the women completely unprepared. One day a few fans might stay after a performance and visit; now there were thousands. Men who had once flirted with them were now sending them revealing photos, writing them love letters, and tossing briefs and boxers onto the stage during con-

certs. The blondes, often sporting the feather boas, platform heels, and fringed bra tops that appeared to have
been stolen from one of Cher's closets, were now being included in thousands of fantasies. Only Shania Twain
seemed to have more male fans, and hers appeared to be
older than the ones who had fallen head over heels for the
Chicks.

One fan wrote as part of a long tribute on one of the
scores of Internet sites devoted strictly to all things Chick:
"The real reason I like them is because they have their own
unique style, and they don't try to be something they are
not. They are just themselves, and I envy them for that."

That "being themselves" is what had turned on so
many thousands of America's youth to the trio. They saw
the Chicks as part of a generation that was not afraid to
rebel and be different. Kids could identify with them. It
was one of the first times in a generation teens had gotten
excited in large numbers about a country music act.

Yet the band's popularity went deeper than teenagers
and young adults liking their looks and sound. For the very
first time, it appeared that each member of the band was
comfortable with their product as well. Shirley Jinkins,
who from her seat at the *Fort Worth Star-Telegram* had
watched the group since their humble beginnings, noted
something very special about the new album. "Unlike the
experimental feel that marked each of the Dixie Chicks'
earlier albums," the DFW scribe wrote, "*Wide Open Spaces*
has a clarity of style and is composition whole."

Jinkins would have been just as accurate if she had
described the band in the same terms. For the first time,
they seemed comfortable and excited about who they were.

Though Martie and Emily had been there through all the transitions, the credit for this new comfort and musical direction had to fall on the shoulders of the diminutive Natalie Maines. She had been the key to taking the talented Erwin sisters to the next level.

The women now found themselves on the cover of every country music magazine, from *Music Row to Country Weekly*. Even *Entertainment Tonight* seemed to be squeezing in reports on the hottest television and movie stars around updates on the Chicks. The television network morning shows wanted them so badly that *Today*, *CBS This Morning*, and *Good Morning America* all offered the women any slot and day they desired to appear. Security guards were not going to toss them out of David Letterman's lobby now, either. Letterman asked for and got the first late-night gig with the Chicks.

Being popular and in great demand also meant having to give up a degree of control over almost every facet of their lives and careers. Now that the Dixie Chicks were performing in front of tens of thousands in huge venues, being mobbed by admirers and pulled a hundred directions at once, they couldn't manage their own affairs. Overnight the trio had been transformed from a novelty act to superstars. So like all superstars, they had to delegate responsibilities.

By and large the team of people who now surrounded the Chicks did a wonderful job addressing all their issues and steering clear of potential problems. However, in one area, the legal forces that had been employed by Monument, as well as the label itself, showed some very poor judgment.

Robert Brooks, who had been such a great fan of the Dixie Chicks almost since their street-corner beginnings, and who had constructed the best Web site devoted to the Chicks, now found himself in the sights of a team of lawyers who didn't like the fact that he was using musical clips of the Chicks and that those clips had been loaded in the MP3 format. MP3, the latest in Web sound, meant that CD-quality clips could easily be downloaded by patrons of the site. Sadly for Brooks, the lawyers probably never would have noticed his additions to his site if he himself hadn't written the Chicks' management to make sure it was all right to put them there. Brooks was hit with an order to pull the plug on all clips—cuts from earlier albums as well as the ones from *Wide Open Spaces*.

The press, who had often used Brooks as a resource on the Chicks, got wind of his legal problems. In a story in the *Dallas Observer*, Monument's desire to bury any images of the old Dixie Chicks became obvious for the first time. "I wanted to show some of the fiddle playing, some of the banjo playing," Brooks had told the *Observer*. "Not even just as an advertisement for their old material, but for their new material, and maybe encourage fans to listen and ask for it, demand that they let those girls play."

The story went on to state that "despite Beiter and Renshaw's legal arguments against Brooks' site, the cease-and-desist letter appears to be part of a broader strategy—constructed by the band, its management, and its label, Sony Music subsidiary Monument Records—to rewrite history, mostly with an eraser, and Brooks' web site is just caught in the middle."

In reading over all the publicity materials being issued

by Monument, the *Observer* noted that Robin Lynn Macy and Laura Lynch were barely mentioned at all. When the two founding Chicks were acknowledged, they were "treated as easily replaceable sidemen who never had much of an impact, other than occupying a place in group photos."

There was a lot of truth in what the Texas newspaper had uncovered. In the official Monument bio the story of just how the Chicks were founded seemed to leave out some important details. In the label's wording, "Emily and Martie begin playing for tips on a Dallas street corner and the duo's debut club appearance at Poor David's Pub." It seemed that the Erwins were just a two-gal family band until they signed up Natalie Maines in 1995.

On his huge Web site Brooks still points out, "Part of what makes them so special to me, and to a lot of people in Dallas I think, is where they've come from and what they've gone through. It's been a long, hard road. To me, that history only serves to enhance what they are now. Without that history, they're just another Shania."

In truth, Monument didn't want any reminders of the Dale Evans Chicks to get in the way of marketing the new Dixie Chicks as a sexy threesome who were after Shania's audience. Though Brooks's page on the Net was allowed to keep running, minus the audio clips, the label was not going to publicize it or anything else that had to do with the Chicks' early period of development. It was rumored that the label was even trying to buy up any unsold copies of the band's first three albums to keep them out of the hands of fans who had just discovered the trio. By midyear 1998, those independent albums were becoming very hard to find. But it sure wasn't hard to find a copy of *Wide Open Spaces*. The new CD and tape were everywhere.

As the women hit Canada on a midyear tour, Anika Van Wyk wrote in the *Calgary Sun*, "Though they can break hearts and set fashion trends just as easily as the Spice Girls, this Girl Power group has real talent." In Canada, as well as in many clubs in the United States, Dixie Chicks concerts were beginning to take on a flavor of a night spent with rockers. Fans were going crazy for the women. Ticket lines would sometimes go for blocks, and thousands would pack rooms meant for hundreds. Before shows, enthusiastic patrons would chant "Chicks Kick Ass!" until the women finally made their appearance on the stage. Police lines were often formed between the stage and the screaming fans just to keep the women from being mobbed. The band was generating the kind of energy and excitement and fanatical worship that Elvis and other teen idols had four decades before. For the cops it was often scary, but for the women, especially Natalie Maines, it was "to die for."

As their fans grew younger and younger and the Chicks' album began to receive play on pop stations, even finding its way into rock's top ten, the press wanted to know if the women were going to make the leap over to pop music. Martie would always put a quick lid on such talk by clearly stating, "We know what our strengths are — and we want to play country music." She was honest in her desire to stick to her country roots. But it seemed the only thing she wanted more than sticking to her country licks was having a number-one single in 1998.

"There's Your Trouble" was a great record and a radio

favorite. It should have flown to the top of the charts. But in spite of all that it had going for it, eight weeks into its run it seemed doomed to finish second. Garth Brooks's "To Make You Feel My Love" was always one step ahead of the women. When Brooks hit number two and the Chicks landed one step back, the battle for the top spot seemed to be decided in the Oklahoman's favor. Martie must have been deeply disappointed. Yet the next week, when *Billboard* issued its latest report, the women had done the impossible: the Chicks had jumped the country music superstar, leaving Brooks stuck again at number two while the DCs grabbed their first chart-topping record with just their second release.

Even though they held *Billboard*'s country chart in their hands, Natalie, Martie, and Emily couldn't believe that they had taken number one away from country music's single most important power. "We jumped him—it was the biggest thing!" Emily told interviewers. It *was* a huge thing, too: few artists had ever jumped over Garth Brooks. Garth, who had already gone on record as being a big fan of the Dallas trio, probably didn't care that much: he had already experienced a few weeks at the top with some of his other releases. But the women still wanted to have some fun with him, so they sent him a bright-red pair of boxing gloves signed, "With love—the Dixie Chicks." The male megastar laughed and kept the gift as a trophy.

Late in the summer four hundred invited guests attended a surprise party their label tossed for the women in Nashville. To cap an evening of fun and laughter, officials from Sony hatched a plastic gold egg to mark the Dixie Chicks' first gold album and first number-one single.

There were still several more months of 1998 to go, and Martie already had realized two seemingly impossible goals.

In August, as the Chicks' crowds continued to grow and their album was still flying off the shelves, the "Wide Open Spaces" single was released. Like the first two singles, it was immediately put in heavy rotation. Pushed by a fever of requests from a new batch of country music fans, young teenage girls, the song would cruise up the charts for three months before peaking at the top of playlists in early November. It would hold the top spot until after Thanksgiving.

Like the early Chicks had once done with a now long-forgotten Christmas release, "Wide Open Spaces" was shipped in limited numbers as a vinyl 45 rpm record too. This version of the band's work would become an instant collector's item.

Around the same time their latest single shipped, the second ballots had come into the Country Music Association's offices. When the CMA announced the finalists for the awards to be presented in late September, the Chicks heard their name spoken not once, but twice: the first time for vocal group of the year, the second for the Horizon award, recognizing new and developing talent. When asked how she felt, Marti Seidel exclaimed, "It looks like I'm three-for three!" She then added, "I have been so blessed."

The nominations represented a real breakthrough for the Dixie Chicks. Emily Erwin noted they had gone "from watching the CMAs last year in the nosebleed seats to nominations this year." It was a strange situation for the new group, but unique situations were becoming the norm for the talented trio.

During a publicity junket in New York, the Dixie Chicks joined two other famous unique "chicks": on RuPaul's show, broadcast on VH1, they vamped with not only the popular and bizarre cross-dressing host but with horror queen Elvira.

Fish Griwkowsky, who wrote about all the acts that interested Canadians, seemed to be composing weekly features on the Dixie Chicks. His colorful prose fully captured the quality that was fueling both the band's success and Shania Twain's too: talent combined with out-front, open and blatant sex appeal. Just who brought that look to the DCs was not lost on him when he proclaimed, "With all due respect, Maines is the kind of gal who makes construction workers' eyes fly right out of their heads. And coincidence or not, ever since she joined it's been all uphill for the trio." *People* magazine, which entered the publicity fray just before the CMAs with a feature on the women, also focused on the women's combination of talent and sex appeal. "Their sweet harmonies — and the way they strut their stuff — have made the Dixie Chicks country's darlings," the popular weekly said.

After listening to and observing the women when they hit the East Coast, the *Washington Post* noted that the trio had "harmonies and attitude to spare." Yet later in the same article came the real gem of understanding: "[The Dixie Chicks] recall the days before Nashville discovered ways of turning out hits with assembly line efficiency."

In a feature for the London, Oregon *Free Press*, Sandra Coulson once again evoked the name of the rock group

Natalie Maines now openly loved to hate. But Ms. Coulson's words scored anyway: "With their Spice Girls—sounding name and cover-girl looks, the Dixie Chicks could be seen as yet another of the music industry's manufactured acts. But consider this: That combination has helped the trio of twenty-somethings from Texas with the bluesy, rocking sound to become the best-selling country group in 1998."

The people of Oregon must have agreed, as they came out sixteen thousand strong to watch the Chicks perform. Just months before, they had been appearing at clubs as unknowns; now they were almost as famous as Mark Chesnutt and Clay Walker, two of the men they had fronted for at several dozen major showcases. It had to have been a mind-blowing experience for the trio to go from working junior highs to record-setting shows in just two years.

Forced to give up their old pink RV, the women now hit the road on a real custom bus. With their lighting and soundmen, plus the other band members, they now had a dozen bodies on the trail with them. By the end of the year they would add a few more men for the more complicated sound and lighting setups, as well as a trailer to haul the equipment needed for the huge stadiums that were now booking them. About the only thing left from their old pink wagon was a disco ball, which they hung on the new bus. With the Dale Evans outfits hiding somewhere in a closet deep in Texas, the ball was about all they had to remind them of the years of struggle before they suddenly became the hottest item in the entertainment world. And still the surprises kept coming.

A year before, they were looking forward to just having

a chance to record their own album; now they were asked to headline on a special CD, *Tribute to Tradition*, a collection of covers of classic country songs. Joining the Chicks would be Randy Travis, Joe Diffie, Martina McBride, and a long list of other top acts. Yet it was the Chicks who got top billing with their cut of "Stand by Your Man."

As big as everything else had been in 1998, it was the CMAs that meant the most. In 1997 the women had bummed seats in the balcony. Now they not only had their own reserved seats, front row center, but they were performing too. They had to have wondered if they were living in a dream world that would suddenly go away. Not even Shania and Garth had risen to the top this quickly. Yet this was no dream, and it was about to get even better.

Emily, the only single Chick left, had somehow found the time to work in a few social outings with Texas songwriter Charlie Robinson and accept a marriage proposal. Yet the wedding would take a backseat to the women's career. At this moment walking down the aisle probably paled in comparison to working the CMAs.

To anyone who asked, the always honest Emily admitted that she was more nervous than she had ever been. So were Natalie and Martie. Yet even though they prayed to hear their name called at least once, the trio didn't honestly think the odds were stacked in their favor. Yet the audience disagreed. Most thought the women would easily pull down the Horizon award for the top new artist or group. In the history of country music, who else had ever done as much right out of the blocks? Of course they won.

Dressed in rather conservative evening wear, the women accepted the Horizon honor with grace and charm.

They were thrilled to be going home with their first award. They didn't expect anything else.

Still, later in the three-hour CBS-TV network special, the women strained to hear their name mentioned with the other nominees in the category of Group of the Year. Most experts believed that the honor would end up in the hands of Alabama or Diamond Rio. Some gave Sawyer Brown an outside shot. The Mavericks, like the Dixie Chicks, had not been picked to finish.

"My heart stopped beating when they called our name!" Emily exclaimed later at a press conference. "I didn't know what to do, and my fiancé started hugging me and saying, 'I'm so proud of you.'"

The shock and joy each of the women felt was apparent as they accepted their trophies. A tearful Martie said, "Thanks for letting us color outside the lines," referring to the fact that country music had accepted the Chicks' unique style and music. For the fiddler, it was a humbling and very satisfying experience.

Emily would later say that "the Horizon award meant so much to us because it means the industry has faith in you and feels like you'll have some longevity." Getting both group and newcomer award in the same night probably meant that not only had the women arrived, but Music City expected them to stick around for a while, too.

The talk at the postawards party was about tattoos. Natalie had made the two original Chicks vow to get a chicken-feet tattoo on their ankles for each number-one record. In August they had each gotten "branded" for the first chart-topping record. Their fans and the media now wanted to know if the women were going to do that for all their awards. Natalie seemed game, but Martie and Emily only promised to think about it.

Meanwhile, Monument had a great deal more to brag about than just their anchor group's CMA awards. In early October *Wide Open Spaces* passed the million sales mark and was certified platinum. It was the fastest any Sony record had ever achieved such a mark.

With their huge successes in both awards and sales, the Chicks' lives grew even more complicated as more demands were placed on them. Rather than complain, the energetic trio got used to performing, racing to airports, sleeping on red-eye flights, doing a national television gig, then catching another flight to their next show. In short order the women appeared on *Regis and Kathie Lee*, *Conan O'Brien*, and *The Tonight Show with Jay Leno*. They also found themselves trying to field magazine interview requests from everyone from *Entertainment Weekly* to *Playboy*.

As the year wound down, the Chicks discovered that they were being honored again. The band was nominated for two awards, Favorite New Country Artists and Favorite Country Band, Duo, or Group, by the American Music Awards. Now the women were going to have to find another set of designer dresses and figure out a way to work a January trip to Los Angeles into their schedules.

For Christmas, Monument found yet one more way to surprise the women and make what had been an incredible year even better. The label had been notified that in just over two months *Wide Open Spaces* had gone from platinum to double platinum. The Chicks were also told that their album would pass the three million sales mark and earn triple-platinum status by early 1999. What a ride! What a year!

In 1995 it had to have been a very tough decision for the Erwins to give up the cowgirl look and their original sound. By hanging on to the bluegrass/retro-western band identity, they would have been assured a long and successful run as Dallas's most popular band. By keeping what they had, the women could have played it safe and made a decent living. But they had decided to make a dramatic change and cross the road to embrace a more marketable sound. By making such a radical move, the Chicks could have lost everything. Instead their gamble won more than they ever dreamed of claiming as their own.

Looking back at the year, Emily latched on to not the gold and platinum records, the number-one singles and videos, or the Group of the Year award as being most important to her. The talented musician told *Dallas Morning News* writer Mario Tarradell that it had been the Horizon award that had the deepest meaning. "[The award] is such an honor because people think you will be around for a while." She then added, "That is what we want. We don't want to be a flash in the pan."

The world is full of former overnight stars who couldn't sustain their initial success. There's even a name for such acts: "one-hit wonders." Could the Dixie Chicks build on a foundation constructed of just a single best-selling album and two years of national exposure? This year had made them rich and famous; the next would determine if they had the talent and drive to stay at the top.

11

Chicks Flying High

The Chicks' Monument debut went gold, platinum, and double platinum faster than any debut album in the history of Sony Nashville. On top of these amazing numbers, *Wide Open Spaces* sold more than two million copies in just nine months, making it the fastest-selling debut album by any group in country music history—and that covered a lot of ground! The Dixie Chicks also became the only country group in the history of Sony Nashville to have a top-ten pop album. At the beginning of the new year their disc had hit number 6 on *Billboard's* Top 200 Albums Chart (Rock), outselling such mainstream artists as 'N Sync and Jay-Z. By the end of the month—January 27, to be precise: the same date *Wide Open Spaces* hit stores in 1998—the record passed not just three million copies in sales but the four million mark too! This was going to be a near-impossible act to follow.

Yet, based on the performance of another hot artist, it could happen. Shania Twain's debut album had hit similar numbers, and the Canadian singer had been able to not only follow up but build on the numbers she garnered the first time out of the box. So, while it would be remarkable, to say the least, for the Dixie Chicks to have a second album score like their first, producing a follow-up that found similar acceptance had been done by another hot newcomer. The Texas songbirds could look to Shania for inspiration.

While the news on the album was better than anyone could have predicted, the question on most people's minds concerned the future. What would the Chicks do now? Just as they had done and were still doing with Twain since her arrival in Music City, many critics and reporters predicted the Dixie Chicks would soon go pop. This belief had gained ground when the bible of rock music trumpeted their work in a late 1998 issue. "The Dixie Chicks were the badass queenpins of country this year, ruling the radio with their crazy sexy cool," *Rolling Stone* declared in its annual wrap-up of the year's best albums. "The Dixie Chicks were country's finest proponents of high-spirited thrills."

Again and again Emily and Martie tried to quash the move-to-rock rumors: "We have no plans to ask any other radio format to play our records. Country music is our heritage, it's what we are, and what we will continue to be." Still, in the face of being lionized by a growing teen audience, the trio simply couldn't still every voice or answer every question. They were just going to have to let their music and live shows talk for them.

Dick Clark, who had witnessed his share of teen idols, professed a deep fascination with the Dixie Chicks. He liked them and was impressed with their talent. Early in the year he had even spent a few days around the trio, and America's Oldest Living Teenager shared his impressions with *Country Weekly* of the group's marketing potential based on their name alone. "What a wonderful idea!" Clark had said. "Dixie Chicks is totally politically incorrect, but the alliteration of Dixie and Chicks goes together." The man who all but invented teen marketing knew that the name first picked by a much different Chicks band might have been hokey a decade ago but was perfect for the 1999 market.

Others thought so too. Candies shoes, a manufacturer that sold in huge numbers to teens and young women, signed the Dixie Chicks up as the company's national spokespeople. Not only was the endorsement worth a chunk of change for the Chicks' pockets, but they got all the new shoes they wanted and lots of new publicity.

General Motors and George Strait decided that they had better hurry and sign the women up for the George Strait Chevy Tour. Once again the Chicks' deal scored big numbers for their bankers and investors.

Yet not everything was rosy for the women in the band. On January 25, 1999, the press got wind of the fact that Natalie Maines had filed for divorce eleven days earlier. Over the course of their short marriage, Michael Tarabay had probably seen less of Natalie than had many of the singer's loyal fans. He certainly hadn't gotten to spend the time with her that the members of the Chicks' tour group had. It seemed that Hank Williams Jr.'s observations about choosing between a career and a family were right on in this case. Long ago Williams had warned anyone thinking about getting into the entertainment business that it was all but impossible to make a success of both at the same time. Maines was just another in a long line of country music stars to prove him right.

While the divorce might have hurt Natalie, it didn't seem to slow the Chicks down at all. Hot Texas performer Neal McCoy told *Country Weekly* in an issue that hit newsstands the same day Natalie's divorce was made public, "The Dixie Chicks are the latest example of the level of talent coming from the Lone Star State. The Chicks are on fire and deservedly so." But could they get any hotter than they already were? The answer appeared to be "Yes!"

About a month later the Chicks hit the top ten with their fourth release from *Wide Open Spaces*. "You Were Mine," a song the label had not really wanted to use as a single, was turning out to be a crowd favorite. The Erwin sisters were now admitting that the song's lyrics dealt with the breakup of their parents' marriage, something that happened only after the sister Chicks had left the nest. Yet as she sang the sad number in live shows, it seemed that the newly divorced Natalie could identify strongly with the song as well.

Also in February, *TV Guide* hopped onto the women's bandwagon. "The trio's broad blend of influences has resulted in a distinctive style," the publication declared in its February 20 issue. "With Seidel and Erwin firmly rooting the band's sound in traditional instrumentation, and with

Maines providing an energetic and thoroughly modern spark, the Dixie Chicks are proving that country music can move forward while maintaining a link to its past."

The Chicks—whose album had taken the Canadian-born Twain's second release on for a year and had at least managed to run the beauty a dead heat in the United States—now were even hotter than Shania north of the border. Almost 500,000 copies of their album had sold in Canada alone, proving the women from Texas were keeping a lot of fans warm in snow country.

Many in Music City thought it might be time for the Chicks to cut back a little on their off-the-wall fashion statements and begin to play it safe in Faith Hill–type clothes. After all, opening for George Strait meant that they would be playing to a much older crowd than the kids who had caught their act the year before. Yet rather than cut back on their "excesses," the women magnified them. Their outfits became more formfitting and outlandish, and Natalie continued to lead chants on stage and say whatever popped into her head. Martie, the mature Chick, even streaked her blond hair with pink highlights.

At the Grammys in March, the Chicks tried in vain to explain why their wild look and unpredictable stage performances worked so well in country music. After the show Emily told Robyn Flans of *Country Weekly*, "Our music is fairly traditional, but our clothes are just another way to express ourselves. We don't wear things to match our music. We just want to do the unexpected with what we're wearing." At the award show, Natalie's short flapper skirt and low-necked top, Martie's midriff-baring two-piece skirt and top (along with sandals that seemed to be constructed largely of barbed wire), and Emily's bullfighter-like outfit caught everyone's attention. So did the dark streaks in the trio's blond locks. The look, wild even by Chick standards, almost eclipsed the fact the women won Grammy Awards for Best Country Album and Best Country Vocal Performance by a Duo or Group. Yet, even though they upset Shania for the former Grammy, they still thought the Canadian had outdressed them with her splashy number than revealed almost all of her flat stomach. The Texas trio also gave Twain credit for opening country music up to women, hot new sounds, and wild sexy clothes.

A few weeks later a reporter from the *Boston Globe* finally got past asking questions about their Grammy evening wear and asked what the awards meant to the group. "That (the award for Best Country Album) was truly shocking," Erwin explained. "But it helped us gain a lot of credibility outside of country music, too. And that's kind of cool."

After the Grammy show the trio could also celebrate their third number-one single. "You Were Mine" did more than just top the playlists; it helped keep the Chicks solidly in charge of the top spot in the country album charts for the second full month in a row.

On nights when the women were opening for George Strait, many solidly conservative middle-American country fans found themselves sitting by tattooed teens dressed in the same kind of wild and colorful clothes embraced by the band. While many Strait fans must have been shocked at first—by both the women and their exuberant fans—by the end of their almost hour-long set the Chicks often had aging baby boomers standing up and shouting "Chick Power!" along with the high schoolers.

There were many who questioned why the Dixie Chicks were opening for anyone. After all, only Shania was as hot as they were. So why hadn't the band chosen to be the headliner on a different package tour? But the women honestly didn't feel they were ready to headline in huge arenas yet. They felt that they didn't have enough material to perform for two hours. They also wanted to work with veterans and watch the way these seasoned professionals managed a crowd. So while the trio might already have sold five million albums and could claim three number-one singles, they didn't think they knew everything. They still saw themselves as having a lot to learn. They figured that working with a master like George Strait was one way to grow into being a headliner.

"We have a diverse fan base, but because of the way we look, some of the older parents don't know what we are," Maines told *USA Today* writer Edna Gundersen in March. "We're getting a chance to prove ourselves to a new audience. Also, we like the challenge of trying to connect to people in the very back rows. It's not easy."

Finally, as Emily explained in another interview, "The George Strait tour is a perfect opportunity to get in front of an average of 50,000 people a night and turn them on to our music, so next year we can hopefully get those same people back. Right now, it's great to just play one hour a night and go knock 'em dead and then hang out with all the other artists the rest of the day. You're not having to worry about the catering, the promotion and everything else. It's somebody else's problem and somebody else's headache. I love it."

Not having the responsibility of being the headline act gave the women a chance to think about their next album, too. Being just a part of the show gave them the time not only to listen to scores of demos, but to write new material of their own on the tour bus and backstage between shows. Earning a number one with a Chick-written cut had given them the drive and confidence to pull from their own experiences for the next album as well.

One of the best experiences they were now feeling was being loved. Even if their show was just an hour long, and even if they weren't the closer, their concert reviews were almost always better than any other performer's on the night's bill. Jerry Sharpe wrote, "The Dixie Chicks were so popular that the fans jumped up as soon as the act was announced. The Chicks didn't disappoint for high energy as Emily Erwin picked her banjo, Martie Seidel fiddled and lead singer Natalie Maines joined in to harmonize 'Tonight the Heartache's on Me.' As pink boas hung from their microphones, the women alternated between ballads, including the hit 'You Were Mine,' and rockers. They even did an old fiddle/banjo instrumental as three male band members danced in women's wigs and men's boxer shorts."

Because of their continued success — at the Grammys, on radio, in concerts, and in sales — to keep the press and public excited Monument wanted to release a second album by September. The label also promised that this new project would not be a huge departure from *Wide Open Spaces*. The powers at Sony reasoned it would be best to stick with a proven formula. Yet the Chicks seemed intent on using the next album as they had the first, to display their growth. So there seemed to be no guarantees as to what direction the final project would take.

One tune, called "Sin Wagon," co-written by Natalie and Emily, was also causing a lot of problems for Sony. They didn't like the message it might be sending to the band's teenage fans. Maines didn't seem to care much about the message of a song that she described as "about a girl who's been good for way too long and she goes out and does all her sinning in one night." All she knew was that their crowds loved it. Natalie appeared to believe the next album was for the fans. If the fans didn't like the message of a song, then they would let the Chicks know it when they tried it out during their show. And the fans had already let the Chicks know they liked "Sin Wagon."

Behind closed doors Monument officials must have known that the Chicks were going to be the Chicks, and that there wasn't really much the label could do about it as long as they were selling millions of albums. At this moment, the women had the power to pretty much decide what went on the next album and what their singles would be. Each of them also had the power to determine her own direction in life. Natalie might have started the year with a divorce, but Emily was determined to end her single status the first weekend in May. On the first day of the month, at the Cibolo Creek Ranch in Big Bend, Texas, the tall blonde married Charlie Robinson. The service took place in a large courtyard, and the Chicks performed "Cowboy, Take Me Away" for the new groom. For a while the wedding seemed steeped in typical grace and charm, unlike anything folks had come to expect from the Dixie

Chicks. But the politeness ended when Natalie and Martie talked all the bridesmaids into jumping into the Jacuzzi with their dresses on. Before the night was over, half the guests ended up in the pool or the Jacuzzi with the Chicks. It was so unexpected that it should have been predicted. It was wild Chicks being wild Chicks.

"When your bridesmaids end up in the Jacuzzi with their dresses on," Emily told *Country Weekly*, "it's a good party."

Less than a week later the Chicks arrived at the Academy of Country Music Awards show in Los Angeles dressed to the nines in pink, blue, and orange. Though their outfits were bright and showy, the clothing was much more conservative than what they had worn to the Grammys. Their hair wasn't streaked, either. To many critics this proved the trio understood that marketing changed based on who was watching you on a given night. The Grammy TV audience was young and hip, and the Chicks had fit in with them. At the ACMs the viewers were older and more conservative, so the Chicks showed a lot less skin and looked a great deal more like the girls next door. Still, they stood out and stood apart, winning three ACM awards, for Duet or Group, New Group or Duet, and Album. Only Faith Hill made more trips to the winner's platform than Natalie, Martie, and Emily. The band had come a long way from the year before, when they had been asked to sing a tribute to Tammy Wynette and then disappear.

Back in Nashville, the women not only worked on their next album but showed Matchbox 20 around town. The country band and the rockers hit a number of clubs and hot night spots, partying until long after most patrons had gone home.

At about the same time the Chicks were being seen with Matchbox 20, they had sneaked into a recording studio to sing on Asleep at the Wheel's latest tribute to Bob Wills and His Texas Playboys. *Ride with Bob* had already captured the sounds of Reba McEntire singing "Right or Wrong," Tim McGraw performing "Milk Cow Blues," Lee Ann Womack tackling "Heart to Heart Talk" and Steve Wariner and Vince Gill jamming with guitars; but once the Chicks climbed on board, it seemed that all the other acts faded into the background. The trio covered the Wills' classic party number, "Roly Poly." For many fans of the original Chicks, this cut might have offered a chance to hear strains of the group that had once played on a Dallas street corner. Yet in truth, even when Robin Lynn Macy and Laura Lynch had sung lead, Texas swing music had not been nearly as big an influence as bluegrass.

While hopeful fans of the original Chicks waited for July and the release of Asleep at the Wheel's new project, they could see and read about the Dixie Chicks in *Country Weekly, Country Music,* and *Music City News,* and also in *Harper's Bazaar, In Style,* and *Seventeen.* Working with Strait as well as on two other major tours, the women seemed to be everywhere at once. The band even announced a planned summer trip to Europe. It wasn't like their first overseas tour several years before: this time the country music fans across the Atlantic knew who the Dixie Chicks were.

The European tour was a big deal, because Sony wanted to take the women to a worldwide audience. When they left in June, the Texas trio would become the first American country act the company had ever sent to Europe. Yet Sony didn't feel they were risking very much with this seemingly radical move. Epic's United Kingdom director of promotions. Adrian Williams, told the CMA's official magazine, *Close Up*, "While some artists and music may not appeal to a broad international audience, the Dixie Chicks are the exception. They have sexiness, sassiness, great songs and they can play. Everybody who's seen them in the UK company is incredibly excited. It doesn't matter where you're coming from musically, everybody gets it."

The women were going to appear at London Shepherd's Bush Empire and Dublin's Olympia Theater, then move across the English Channel to Europe. Just days after the shows were announced, and more than two months before the Chicks left the States, most of the seats had been sold. It seemed the women some were calling America's Spice Girls were about to show their British counterparts what American style and excitement was all about. Before the trio returned to the States, Natalie, who was the weariest of the Spice Girl comparisons, seemed intent on making sure that at least one English writer called the Spice Girls England's answer to the Dixie Chicks.

As they planned for their June departure to Europe, the Chicks finished up their tour of America's biggest stadiums with the massive George Strait Country Music Festival. The women only stopped performing to work a bit on their next album and spend a day with Vice President Al Gore. Gore and the Chicks appeared at the annual memorial service honoring peace officers slain in the line of duty. Following the Veep's remarks, the group performed "Lonesome Road."

The European tour caused the Chicks to miss both Fan Fair 1999 and the *Music City News*/TNN Country Music Awards. Even though they were out of sight, country music fans didn't forget them. Along with Anita Cochran, Sara Evans, the Kinleys, and Lila McCann, the Chicks were nominated for Female Stars of Tomorrow. They won. They also beat out Alabama, Black Hawk, Diamond Rio, and Sawyer Brown for Best Vocal Band. The only award the Chicks were nominated for and failed to win was Best Album. Touring partner George Strait won that honor with *One Step at a Time.*

Though the women couldn't accept their honors on June 14, winning the pair of awards might have been the most important bit of news the Chicks had received in what had been a wonderful first half of 1999. The Country Awards are the result of TNN viewers and *Music City News* readers voting for their favorite acts. The voters in this contest tend to be older and more conservative than those who had picked the Chicks at the Grammys and ACMs. The fact that even the more traditional country music fans had picked the Dixie Chicks for two large honors spoke well for the band's future. Not only did kids and Gen-Xers love them, so did the old-line country guard.

When the Chicks finally came home from Europe, they would hit the road for three months with the Tim McGraw tour and work with Lilith Faith. They would also return to the studio to decide the final direction for their second album. As it drew nearer, it was the recording work that seemed to scare the women much more than the big tours. As Emily said on several occasions, "The scariest part is not screwing up what you're doing right, and sometimes you don't know what it is." Natalie echoed those fears by talking about the "sophomore scare thing," Bryan White had just recently taken a huge fall with his second album, so her fears seemed legitimate, too.

What Natalie, Martie, Emily, and Monument all realized was the future for the hottest act in country music would be largely determined by the caliber of the next album. Even though they had already earned more awards and money than they had ever dreamed was possible, the Chicks didn't want to fall as quickly as they had risen to the top.

As Martie looked into the future, she told *Close Up*, "I still see us touring, and still doing what we're doing, but maybe with some luxury. Maybe with our own tours instead of opening for other people. Maybe calling a little more shots at the label. Making some more decisions that we can't make at this time. Maybe some more chicken feet tattoos on our feet."

The tattoo artists probably have a lot more work to do, as do the folks who make awards and stock records. The Dixie Chicks have helped dramatically change country music in the little more than two years they have been invited to play the game on the national level. In 1995, when the Erwins asked Maines to join them, women ruled country music's top spot only fifteen percent of the time. In 1998, when the Chicks' singles broke out, the percentage of time that females controlled the number-one position had risen to almost half. In the first half of 1999, thanks in large part to the Dixie Chicks, women owned the chart almost seventy percent of the time. This dramatic playlist change, coupled with more than six million units now sold of *Wide Open Spaces*, seems to indicate the Dixie Chicks are dramatically altering the way country looks at women.

As they face the release of the second album, the Chicks find themselves in a spot similar to the one that Alabama had occupied in 1981. Country music's first successful male band not only defeated the sophomore jinx, but went on to earn forty more number-one singles, a shelfful of awards, and tens of millions in album sales, as well as open the door for dozens of country music bands. When RCA first signed them, no one would have predicted that kind of success for Alabama. No one could have predicted the manner in which the band changed country music, either.

The Chicks now have the potential not only to follow Alabama's successes on the charts and at the award shows, but also to throw open the doors for a wave of new female bands. All the Chicks need to do is stay fresh, focused, and hungry. With the well-grounded Martie and Emily making sure the band stays on track, and the unpredictable Natalie looking for new ways to push the envelope, there is reason to bet on a long tenure in country for the Dixie Chicks and a wave of hungry women pickers following them to success in Music City. That would probably thrill even Dale Evans, though the Queen of the West might still prefer the band's original look to the new "trashy" Chicks'.

The Dixie Chicks are one of only a handful of country music artists who really do hold their future in their own hands. They have created their look, their sound, and their success. If they stay confident but humble, continue to recognize and play to the most loyal segment of the huge fan base, and stay hungry even after they have built their dream houses and have millions in the bank, then they can continue to tour and wow audiences for the next twenty years. The only thing besides the current fickle nature of country music (and major acts such as Alabama, George Strait, and Garth Brooks have survived in this fickle climate) that might stand in their way is having to choose between a life devoted to hits and time spent with their families. However, if anyone can figure out how to have it both ways, it will be the Dixie Chicks.

The band Music City had trouble accepting for so many years has now been embraced by the world. Not only has that been good for the Dixie Chicks, but it has been wonderful for music growth in Nashville.

Chick Power is a great thing!